# OVERVIEW

**Overview**
**Building Rapport in Customer Relationships**

Keeping customers satisfied and ensuring they return to your company requires that you're focused on your customers. To focus on your customers, you need to pay them your full, undivided attention and minimize interruptions to your interactions with them.

To focus on customers, you also need to connect with them. Finding commonalities helps establish connections, which are created and nurtured through communication and relationship building.

Finally, a positive and friendly attitude is helpful. By having a good attitude, you reduce stress in yourself and in others. You also need to offer positive solutions to customers' problems. In each case, either come up with a practical solution or validate and recognize the personal nature of the customer's problem.

Empathy enables you to connect with customers and build good relationships with them. Empathy involves listening to, understanding, and validating customers' feelings. Three techniques you can use to demonstrate empathy are to relate your own experience, reflect people's emotions, and to normalize their responses.

Relating your own experiences is a way of reassuring customers that you have some understanding of their situations, and places you on equal footing with them. To be effective, keep your stories brief and relevant.

Reflecting customers' emotions and problems back to them can be a very effective way to convey understanding and shows a desire to be helpful. As such, it is a good way to set distressed customers at ease and address their problems effectively.

Normalizing responses lets customers know their problems are normal and reassures them that they don't need to be hard on themselves for getting upset.

When you build rapport, your customers feel valued and value their business with you. They're more likely to return to you and are likely to speak to others about the service they receive.

The strategies you can use to build rapport at each phase of the customer relationship include paying attention, connecting with the customer, showing empathy, and being positive.

**Internal Customer Service**

Although only some people in a company deal directly with external customers, the way colleagues interact has an impact on the external customers' experience of the company's services. Colleagues should think of each other as internal customers and internal customer service providers.

Identifying internal customer service relationships involves analyzing work relationships. Your internal customers are the colleagues who rely on you to get their work done and your internal customer service providers are the colleagues who you rely on.

Companies often implement initiatives on an organizational level to promote understanding and cooperation between departments. However, individuals can also take responsibility for improving their internal customer service.

This process involves listing your internal customers, getting to know their work processes and roles within the organization, discussing your mutual expectations openly, and implementing any necessary action. The final step involves getting feedback and reviewing the process so as to constantly improve internal customer service.

Developing an internal customer service attitude is the first and most important step to improving internal customer service.

It involves learning to see oneself as a service provider and taking pride in that role, using common courtesy to create a healthy atmosphere in the workplace, and looking for opportunities to exceed the expectations of internal customers.

**Customer Service in the Field**

The on-site customer service process consists of five stages – preparation, arrival, service, wrap up, and follow up. Following specific guidelines during each of these stages can ensure that you provide professional, high-quality service that leaves customers satisfied.

Visits to customers pose specific challenges because they require you to make use of effective interpersonal skills.

Four guidelines help ensure your visits are a success. Starting on a positive note sets the tone for the visit and establishes a personal connection with the customer. When setting expectations, you let your customer know what you're there to do and how long it'll take. Active listening involves fully focusing on what the customer says, demonstrating your understanding, and asking for clarification whenever necessary. You help customers understand your products by explaining your products or services in a way that's easy to understand, patiently, and without using jargon.

To provide service excellence with customers you meet on site, you should start your meeting on a positive note, set clear expectations, listen actively, and help your customers understand your products.

When you apply these strategies, your customers will be impressed with the quality of your service.

**Customer Service over the Phone**

By applying basic rules of telephone etiquette, you ensure you project a professional image over the phone. Specific rules apply for answering a call, putting a customer on hold, transferring a call, and closing a call.

To deliver outstanding customer service over the telephone, you can use several techniques.

These include minding your tone of voice, listening actively to the customer, using customer-focused language, using a range of problem-solving strategies to resolve the customer's problems, and mirroring a customer's language.

These strategies help you to put customers at ease, facilitating positive, successful interactions in each call you handle.

## Customer Service Confrontation and Conflict

Very often, helping complaining customers isn't just about finding solutions for problems. It may also involve defusing their feelings of frustration.

Instead of trying to avoid responsibility for a problem, you should try to be helpful, take ownership of the problem, and act as your customers' point of contact for resolving it.

You should avoid setting unrealistic expectations. Don't criticize your company, colleagues, products or services. Rather apologize, promise to investigate incidents, and focus on offering solutions rather than on how problems arose.

Allow your customers to vent their frustrations and respond with empathy and understanding, validating their emotions. Give customers the benefit of the doubt and save differences of opinion for discussion once they are feeling calmer.

The first step in handling customers' complaints is to defuse the frustration by allowing the customers to vent, listening with empathy, and focusing on the customers through active listening.

The next step is to investigate the complaint by asking specific questions, taking responsibility for helping, generating a variety of potential solutions, and getting back to your customer if necessary.

Step three in the process is agreeing on a solution. Make a point of offering alternatives. Welcome suggestions from your customer, but don't lose control of the conversation. Set reasonable expectations, and don't make promises you can't keep.

The final step is to follow up with your customer to ensure the solution worked. If appropriate, you should also follow up with your company to address faulty processes or procedures.

Handling customer complaints effectively fosters good customer relationships and improves your company's image and reputation. It demonstrates care for your customers and the desire to fix any mistakes. By defusing a customer's frustration, investigating the problem, agreeing on a solution, and following up on complaints, you provide excellent customer service.

## Shaping the Direction of Customer Service in Your Organization

Moments of truth are the defining moments in the interaction with a company that leave an impression on the customer. In order to manage these moments and create a positive experience for the customer, you need to adopt a systematic approach.

The first step is to map the customer's experience and divide it into segments, and then identify the crucial moments from each segment.

You would then research the customer's perceptions in order to find out what they would consider good service. Next you would take action to improve any problem areas in order to turn negative moments into positive ones.

Finally you should plan regular reviews to make sure problems don't resurface, and to take any changes in customers' needs and feelings into account.

All companies should have both service visions and service standards. Standards are closely aligned with service visions. If properly maintained, they make your company reliable so that your customers can expect service consistency.

To create and implement service standards, you follow a simple three-step process. First you identify all instances of customer interaction – service steps – and break them down into the sub-steps forming each interaction. Then you pinpoint elements that enhance the customer experience of each interaction. Finally, you convert these elements into specific, action based, observable and customer centric service standards.

In order for a business to stay ahead of changes in its operating environment, it needs to implement a dynamic customer service strategy and it needs to remain focused on the customers' changing needs.

To develop an effective service strategy, a business must carry out four steps. First it needs to carry out a situational analysis, then it needs to identify its targets and value, and then it needs to implement that value. The final step is to remain in tune with customers' ever changing needs. This can be achieved by implementing and using Customer Relationship Management systems, by monitoring, analyzing and responding to customers' feedback, by gathering and reviewing information from word of mouth, and by creating dedicated customer insight teams.

# CHAPTER ONE
*Building Rapport in Customer Relationships*

**Paying attention**

Customers tend to form judgments of your company based on the quality of their interactions with the people working there. If the first person a customer encounters on walking into your shop is an unfriendly assistant, the customer won't feel welcome, attended to, or comfortable. This first impression will often persist even if every other staff member is friendly and provides excellent service.

Another common pitfall is when you're so absorbed in your duties that you consider customers as distractions – or even annoyances. Every company, or individual, is accountable to people who pay for goods and services. So, without them, your job couldn't exist.

Finding new customers is far more difficult and expensive than keeping existing customers. Also, customers tell others about the type of service they receive. News of bad service damages your organization, reduces profits, and may eventually cost everyone their jobs.

If customers receive good service, they will advertise on behalf of your business is likely to grow.

So how do you create a positive experience for your customers? The secret of excellent customer service lies in your ability to focus on the customer. Being customer-focused helps you build rapport, which in turn leads to solid, positive, gratifying customer relationships. When you focus on your customers, you show them they are important to you and you make them feel special.

Your customer-focused attitude should be consistent across the phases of building relationships with your customers, whether you are meeting them for the first time or trying to cultivate and maintain relationships with them.

A few simple strategies help you to be customer-focused and to provide excellent customer service. To demonstrate you're focused on your customers, you need to give them your full, undivided attention, connect with them, and remain positive in your dealings with them.

See each strategy to find out more about it.

**Give your undivided attention**

Good customer service involves paying real attention to what customers want. If you don't pay attention, you can't be sure of what customers want from you, or whether you're satisfying their needs.

Additionally, giving your full attention to people lets them know that you value them and take their needs and wants seriously.

**Connect with your customers**

Connecting is necessary for meaningful, satisfying interactions with customers and can be accomplished in many different ways.

When you feel connected to someone, you feel respected, cared for, and comfortable with that person.

People feel connected to you when they can identify with you or feel that you share something in common with them.

**Be positive**

Being positive is about being pleasant and affirming to interact with. It's also about finding effective ways to help people and offering constructive solutions for customers' problems.

How can you demonstrate to a customer that he has your full and undivided attention? The answer is quite simple – stop what you're doing and give your whole attention to the customer. If you're interrupted while speaking with your customer, deal with the interruption quickly and focus on your customer again.

See each action to find out more about how to be truly attentive with customers.

**Stop what you're doing**

When a customer approaches you, it's important that you stop whatever it is that you're doing at the time. This shows the customer that he has your full, undivided attention.

For example, you should put down whatever is in your hands at the time, turn away from your computer, or close any open files or books.

**Deal with interruptions quickly**

Try to avoid being interrupted when interacting with a customer. If interruptions can't be avoided, deal with them as quickly as you can.

For example, if you're busy with a customer, and you're forced to answer the phone, explain to the customer that you'll simply take the caller's details and return to him. And then do just that.

**Connecting and being positive**

Once your customer has your full attention, you need to find ways to connect with her. Connecting with people is all about establishing a relationship. Relating to people is easiest when you identify with them or recognize your commonalities.

To nurture connections with customers you need to find commonality with them. You also need to say things that make people feel welcome and that assure them they mean something to you.

See each strategy for examples of behaviors that help you connect with customers.

**Find commonality**

A good way of connecting with people is to find things that you have in common with them. This helps customers to identify with you and to feel comfortable relating to you.

To find commonalities, you need to listen actively to your customer with a genuine interest and concern. And you need to pay attention to the customer's feelings, meaning, intentions, and body language.

When you find something you have in common, you can communicate this to your customer, if appropriate. For example, you could comment on the fact that both of you are left handed.

**Make people feel welcome**

Making people feel welcome is an important way of connecting at all stages of building a relationship. Whenever you come across customers, you should do something to make them feel welcome.

At first contact, or when a customer has just entered your premises, it's important to greet him. Smiling at people is one of the most effective ways to make people feel welcome without needing to speak.

For example, when a customer first walks in to a room, he may feel ill at ease. If you smile at him, even without greeting him, he feels acknowledged. He now knows he isn't intruding and is welcome to be in the room.

**Show that people mean something to you**

When you mean something to another person, you feel cared for and recognized. You know somebody else thinks about you.

To show customers that they mean something to you, you should learn their names and use them whenever appropriate, such as when you greet or call them.

Remembering information such as customers' likes and dislikes or their personal details, gives your connection history and significance. Making eye contact and actively listening also convey that other people are important to you.

## Customer Service Fundamentals

For instance, if you know your customer loves antiques, you can call him about some pieces you think he may like. This shows your customer that he matters to you.

Angela is a regular customer at an upmarket clothing boutique. Follow along as Sara tries to establish a good connection with Angela by helping her find what she is looking for.

**Sara:** Good morning Angela, how are you today?

**Angela:** Very well. Although I'm a bit worried that I won't find just what I need for our work team-building weekend.

**Sara:** I also battle to find the right thing sometimes. What is it that you're looking for exactly?

**Angela:** I need a new summer dress. Light, comfortable, not too revealing.

**Sara:** We've just got new stock in for the summer. You usually look for simple cuts and natural fabrics, right?

**Question**

What does Sara do to establish a connection with Angela?

**Options:**

1. She greets Angela by name and smiles at her
2. She remembers what kinds of clothes Angela usually buys
3. She pays close attention to Angela and responds to her anxiety about finding the right thing
4. She compliments Angela appropriately
5. She listens actively by asking Angela for more information about her team-building weekend

**Answer:**

Option 1: This option is correct. By using her customer's name and smiling at her, Sara makes Angela feel welcome and important.

Option 2: This option is correct. Sara remembers Angela likes simple cuts and natural fabrics. Consequently, Angela feels that Sara is interested in her choices and that their interactions are meaningful.

Option 3: This option is correct. By relating her own anxiety, Sara helps Angela identify with her.

Option 4: This option is incorrect. Sara doesn't pay Angela any compliments, although complimenting customers is one way to show warmth and caring.

Option 5: This option is incorrect. Although this would be one way to listen actively and connect to Angela, Sara doesn't ask her about her team-building weekend.

The third strategy for focusing on your customers is to be positive and friendly. This attitude projects professionalism and success. It builds and strengthens relationships by making you a pleasant person to do business with.

Do you lose your cool? Do you get cranky and nervous? It's often hard to be positive or friendly in stressful situations. However, it's in these situations that being positive has the most to offer.

Being positive and friendly doesn't make problems go away, but it helps make other people feel better. Staying positive can bring strength and reassurance to others. Stress is thereby reduced, or even eliminated, enabling problems to be tackled more effectively.

Your positivity will reduce your stress levels as well. And, your apparent professionalism will enable you to easily build rapport and strengthen relationships with customers, ensuring that they seek you out for your expertise, positive demeanor, and relaxed approach.

Being positive is more than simply having a good attitude. It's also about offering positive solutions to problems. When you're unable to help a customer, offer an alternative rather than simply saying no. Even when you have to give people bad news, you can still offer positive solutions.

For example, if a customer is searching for a speciality item that you don't normally keep in stock, you could offer to order it for him rather than simply saying that your store doesn't offer it.

**Question**

How often do you find yourself saying "no" to customers or telling them that you can't help? Options:

1. Very often
2. Sometimes
3. Rarely

**Answer:**

Option 1: Naturally, not everyone can be helped all the time. Perhaps your work often involves giving people bad news or otherwise disappointing them.

However, not all problems are practical ones. Sometimes a customer needs to have his feelings or personal issues acknowledged. When you understand a person's problem more accurately, you're better able to suggest a positive solution.

Option 2: As a general rule, try to avoid refusing customer requests. Offering alternative solutions isn't as difficult as it may seem. Once you've identified and understood problems, you may be able to solve them easily.

Option 3: You're probably good at eliciting information from customers about what they actually need and how they're feeling. You also seem able to offer positive solutions to their problems.

When problem-solving, always offer an alternative and reflect the customer's feelings and statements back to him in your responses. Include reflection on the customer's feelings and a solution you can try.

How do you go about giving positive solutions to customer's problems, even when you can't make the problems go away? Follow along as Sara tries to help Margaret.

**Margaret:** You told me the alterations on my dress would be ready today. What am I supposed to wear to the show now?

*Margaret asks angrily.*

Sara: I did tell you they'd be ready, but unfortunately they're not. I know how important the show is so I'll be happy to give you one of our rental dresses for the occasion.

*Sara responds calmly and seriously.*

Margaret: I am so anxious, and this dress has to look just right.

Sara: I know the dress is important to you and I can see it's making you very anxious. Perhaps you could try some of our dresses on right away. We have lots of dresses in your size.

*Sara responds reassuringly.*

Margaret: Thank you so much. I really appreciate your help.

*Margaret responds with relief.*

Sara has offered positive solutions to Margaret's problems. She acknowledges Margaret's feelings, and offers practical solutions. Notice that she repeats Margaret's problems back to her in her answers. The result is that Margaret is reassured that Sara has her best interests at heart.

**Question**

What behaviors demonstrate a customer-focused attitude?

**Options:**

1. When customers walk into the office, Maria always smiles and greets them

2. Frank, a hairdresser, spends a lot of time with his clients looking at haircuts to get a feel for what styles they want

3. Pedro makes a point of looking away from his e-mails whenever he takes a customer query call

4. When a client complains about a late delivery, Gloria says she understands his frustration and offers a discount on his next purchase

5. Pamela always calls her customers "Sir" or "Madam"

6. Tiko loves multi-tasking and often helps several customers at once

**Answer:**

Option 1: This is a correct option. By smiling and greeting customers, Maria makes them feel welcome and establishes a connection with them.

Option 2: This is a correct option. Frank listens actively and pays attention to what his customers actually want. This makes him customer-focused, enabling him to give people haircuts that suit their styles.

Option 3: This is a correct option. By removing the possibility of being distracted by e-mails, Pedro is able to give customers his full attention when they phone him.

Option 4: This is a correct option. By offering solutions to people's problems, Gloria stays positive. This helps her to be customer-focused and build rapport, even with people who seem hard to please.

Option 5: This is not a correct option. Pamela is being polite and formal, rather than connecting with her customers.

Option 6: This is not a correct option. Tiko doesn't give any one customer his full attention, so he can't build good rapport with his customers.

**Empathy**

Think about a time when you were a customer and the employee you were dealing with really listened to you, reassured you, and explained to you what you needed to know. How good did it feel? It is this type of connection that this topic focuses on. With this type of connection, you build rapport and create solid and gratifying customer relationships.

Listening to and understanding a customer's feelings is a fundamental element of rapport. This is known as having empathy. Empathy validates your customers' feelings and shows you really connect with your customers and find them valuable.

Using empathy, you listen for the meaning hidden in your customers' messages, acknowledge their emotions, and provide care to them. This helps customers to feel good about you and about themselves.

To provide empathy sincerely, you need to put yourself in your customers' shoes. This provides insight into their fears, frustrations, confusions, and annoyances, and helps you find a way to put them at ease.

Sincerely acknowledging a customer's negative emotions defuses those emotions. This in turn helps your customer feel better and respond more positively to a difficult situation.

Depending on the situation, there are different approaches to demonstrate you understand your customers' feelings:
- relating your own experience
- showing understanding of what customers are feeling by reflecting their emotions, and
- normalizing their difficulties so they don't feel as though they are the only ones who have ever experienced the problem or situation

**Relating your own experience**

In situations you're familiar with, and where you've experienced similar emotions, it's helpful to share your experiences with your customer. This shows that your interaction is between equals and that you have some expertise in dealing with the issue. However, it's important to keep your story brief and your examples relevant.

See each guideline for more information on how to relate your own experience.

**Keep it brief**

If you tell long and involved stories, you begin to make the situation about you rather than your customer. Also, you show a lack of respect for your customer's time. So when relating your own story, always try to keep it brief.

For example, saying, "I had the same problems when I used my credit card online the first time" is helpful. But relating what you were trying to buy and giving details of the online store and the bargain you could have missed is not very useful.

**Keep it relevant**

Relating your own experience should reflect that you have some expertise in dealing with the issue and that you're on an equal footing with your customer. Because of this, the story you relate should closely resemble the customer's current experience.

For example, if a customer is confused about the requirements for an insurance quote, you should briefly tell your own story about being confused in a similar situation. For instance, you could say, "I had the same problems the first time I asked for an insurance quote."

You don't show empathy when you recount the problems you had while enrolling at college or when you try to convince the customer your experience is worse than his.

Relating your own experience can be used at all stages of customer relationship building.

Suppose a customer enters your store for the first time and is embarrassed because he can't figure out how to operate his digital camera. You can respond to him by saying, "I remember I had the same problem when I switched to that model. Let me explain to you how it works – I'm an expert now!" Then you can walk the customer through the basics.

Relating your own stories helps you find the common ground needed to cultivate and maintain a relationship with a customer.

Scott is a regular customer at a health store. Erika is a sales representative for the store. Follow along as Erika attempts to create empathy by relating her own experience.

***Scott:*** Hello. What would you recommend to help me stop smoking? I can't concentrate and I feel very tired.

*Scott looks stressed and grumpy.*

***Erika:*** Stopping smoking can be really tough. When I stopped, I slept solidly for twelve hours a night. I also had the most terrible food cravings and, boy, was I grumpy. In fact, I had to take a whole week's leave because I just couldn't function at work.

*Erika looks animated.*

***Scott:*** That sounds terrible. Do you have any vitamin supplements or something?

*Scott looks grumpy.*

**Question**

How well do you think Erika shows empathy to Scott's problem while relating her own experience to him?

**Options:**

1. Excellent
2. Fair
3. Poor

**Answer:**

Option 1: You think the way Erika relates her experience that's similar to Scott's is excellent. Remember that you relate your own experience to show that your interaction is between equals and that you have some expertise in dealing with the issue. In Erika's case, she adds unnecessary detail, which turns the focus to her. She also implies that her experience was much worse than Scott's, which is a type of one-upmanship that's far removed from empathy.

Option 2: You think the way Erika relates her experience is fair. However, she fails to use the opportunity to make Scott believe the interaction is between equals. Instead, she implies that her experience was much worse than his, which is a type of one-upmanship that has little to do with empathy. It's also questionable whether she'll be able to help Scott because she adds unnecessary detail, which turns the focus to her.

Option 3: When you rate Erika's response as poor, you're on the right track. Erika doesn't show empathy. Although she relates an experience similar to Scott's to make him feel he's talking with an equal who'll be able to help him quit smoking, she adds unnecessary detail. This turns the focus to her and implies her experience was much worse than Scott's.

**Reflecting emotion**

The second strategy for having empathy is to reflect emotion, or show understanding of why your customer is feeling the way she is. Acknowledging the customer's bad feelings and the reasons behind them is probably the most common way of showing empathy.

To reflect a customer's emotions, you first need to determine what she's feeling. Pay attention to her words, tone of voice, and body language. Do your best to imagine what she may be going through.

Then you acknowledge her feelings and the reasons for them. Reflecting a person's emotions in this way conveys warmth and understanding, and it defuses tension.

Reflecting a person's emotions doesn't require you to agree with her opinions. Instead, you need to understand what matters to her personally. You respond to her situation by reflecting her own statements and feelings. This creates trust between you and shows you empathize with her.

Follow along as Darren talks to a customer service agent, Debora, to complain that his online transaction failed.

**Darren:** I have a complaint to make. My online transaction hasn't gone through. Again.

*Darren says angrily*

**Debora:** That shouldn't happen. I know how frustrating it is when a transaction fails.

**Darren:** I can tell you all about it. I order reference books online, which I need to complete urgent projects. When a transaction fails, my orders are late and I can't do my work.

*Darren looks less grumpy and more animated.*

**Debora:** Not receiving your orders on time is frustrating. I understand having your transactions go through is so important when you're working on urgent projects. I'll look straight away into the problem to make sure it won't happen again.

*Debora looks calm.*

**Darren:** OK, thanks for your help.

By reflecting Darren's situation and the reason for his feelings, Debora demonstrates empathy. She also offers her help promptly, promising she'll find a solution. As a result, Darren feels taken seriously and acknowledged. He feels understood and genuinely helped.

Suppose Debora had said, "I don't understand why you're frustrated – many transactions don't go through with our new system." In this scenario, she would have acknowledged the emotion but not shown understanding of it. This does not convey empathy. Also, Debora would have sent a negative message about the company's system and made a negative judgment about her customer.

Similarly, a response such as, "I don't understand why you're blaming us. Really, you should have had a plan B," blames the customer for what has happened and doesn't offer understanding or caring service.

**Normalizing difficulties**

When customers are self-critical, or make negative statements about themselves, it's important to offer them reassurance and affirmation that they are not alone. Normalizing a customer's reaction to the difficulty they are experiencing is a way of letting the customer know it's normal to have these problems and feelings in their situation.

When attempting to normalize a customer's response, however, you must be careful to convey the feeling that "they are not alone" rather than implying "they are just like everyone else." It can be a fine line as illustrated by this example.

Suppose a customer calls in because she's unable to figure out how to set up a blog. Select each employee to find out how they respond to the customer's difficulty.

**Catherine**

"Many people feel confused and intimidated when they first try to set up a blog. It's normal to be anxious when working with something new to you."

**John**

"I can't tell you how many times I've heard those exact same words from customers. Just yesterday, Lee said that he spent hours trying to figure it all out. He ended up asking a colleague to help him out."

Catherine's response normalizes the customer's feeling of anxiety, because she makes the customer feel like "she's not alone". She implies that it's a reasonable response to a new situation.

Although John is trying to normalize the customer's difficulties, his words may not have the desired effect. By saying he's heard the exact words many times, he gives the impression that the customer is just like everyone else, making the same mistakes and not able to figure it out without help. This is a bit different from making her feel that she is not alone.

Sometimes people try to normalize responses by talking about other customers' personal experiences. Because John uses another customer's name, it could make the customer feel as though he'll speak about her in the same way. This can actually reduce trust and rapport.

**Question**

What statements demonstrate empathy?

**Options:**

1. "I understand that you're frustrated, but others think our service is great."

2. "I also have trouble estimating accurate arrival times because the unpredictable traffic patterns."

3. "I realize you must be disappointed with the long waiting time. Let me find out exactly when it'll be ready."

4. "I don't think you're being fussy. It's an important decision, so it's sensible to think about it from all angles."

5. "Many find this process intimidating. It's normal to feel nervous when you're confronted with legal jargon."

6. "A lady came in yesterday and was almost in tears because nothing would fit her either."

**Answer:**

Option 1: This option is incorrect. The customer's feelings are being reflected, but not normalized. Instead, the customer is being criticized for having them. Therefore, this statement does not demonstrate empathy.

Option 2: This option is correct. By relating your own experience, you demonstrate empathy and put yourself and your customer on equal footing.

Option 3: This option is correct. Reflecting the customer's feeling of disappointment shows empathy and helps the customer to feel understood and taken seriously.

Option 4: This option is correct. By countering the customer's self-criticism, you normalize his concerns and offer reassurance.

Option 5: This option is correct. By reminding the customer that it is normal to feel intimidated or nervous, and that this is a reasonable response to the situation, you normalize difficulties and demonstrate empathy.

Option 6: This option is incorrect. By relating another customer's negative experience, you make the customer feel that she too would be discussed behind her back. This does not demonstrate empathy.

**Rapport building**

Building rapport is part of good customer service and is crucial for generating customer satisfaction and retention. And by building rapport with customers, you add a human touch to your day-to-day interactions with them.

When you build rapport, your customers feel valued as people and they value their business with you. They're also more likely to return to you when they feel you've established a connection with them.

Another great benefit is that customers advertise their positive experiences with you by talking to others about it. This brings in new customers and helps you keep existing customers.

**Question**

What are the benefits of building rapport with customers?

**Options:**

1. Your customers appreciate you for valuing them as individuals, not simply as people who'll buy from you

2. Your customers tend to return to you because they feel you're connecting with them

3. Your customers remember positive interactions with you and talk about you to other potential customers

4. Your customers are less likely to complain if a product is faulty

5. Your customers are more likely to bad-mouth your competition if they feel loyalty toward you

**Answer:**

Option 1: This is a correct option. People generally like to feel valued for themselves, rather than for their financial worth.

Option 2: This is a correct option. When you connect with people, you form a bond with them. This causes people to return to you.

Option 3: This option is correct. Good relationships give rise to positive interactions. And people discuss their experiences with others – whether they're positive or negative.

Option 4: This option is incorrect. In fact, many customers may feel less inhibited about complaining once rapport has been established, because they'll feel safer voicing their thoughts to you.

Option 5: This option is incorrect. Some customers may indeed have this reaction, especially in a situation where there aren't many competitors to choose between. However, this won't necessarily reflect well on your company or its products.

**Strategies for building rapport**

The strategies you use to ensure customer focus and demonstrate empathy should be used at each stage of the customer relationship – first contact, cultivation, and maintenance. By using these strategies, you build rapport and maximize your chances of creating positive and lasting customer relationships. You can practice these skills in this topic.

Question

One of the skills you need to have in your "rapport-building toolbox" is the ability to handle more than one person at a time.

You work at a hotel reception desk and frequently have to help many guests at once. How would you go about dealing with many customers during particularly busy times?

**Options:**

1. Save time by working on the computer while helping guests, being sure to smile and make eye contact with those you're unable to help immediately

2. Deal with each guest strictly in sequence, and give each person you interact with your exclusive attention whenever possible

3. Help the people who have the most urgent requests first, and promise guests who interrupt that you'll get to them too

**Answer:**

Option 1: This option is incorrect. You may save time by working on your computer, but you won't be giving your guests sufficient attention. By making eye contact with guests who are waiting, you divide your attention from the person you are supposed to be helping.

Option 2: This is the correct option. If you deal with each guest in sequence, you show that you're fair. By giving each person you interact with your undivided attention, you're able to establish rapport with that person.

Option 3: This option is incorrect. If you help the guests who have the most urgent requests first, you'll neglect others and give them inadequate attention. However, it's useful to promise to get back to people who interrupt you.

# CHAPTER TWO
*Internal Customer Service*

**The customer service chain**

You may deal with customers directly or you may work with colleagues who in turn serve customers. You might even work with people who serve other colleagues who then serve customers. No matter where you're in the chain, you're contributing to the quality of service the customer receives in the end.

Vince works for a delivery company. A customer calls him to find out the status of her order. Vince promises to get right back to her with a definitive answer. But when he phones his colleague, Bill, in the Dispatching Department, Bill rudely tells Vince he doesn't have time to find that information. Now Vince can't call the customer with the information he promised her.

When internal relationships break down, as in Vince's case, the customer service chain is broken. Although his colleague doesn't have direct contact with the external customer, his behavior has a negative impact on her experience of the company. Often, customers' perceptions of a company's service delivery is dependent on the way internal customers are treated.

Think of the colleagues you interact with as internal customers and internal customer service providers who contribute to create products and services that external customers will pay for.

See each element of the customer service chain for more information about it.

**Internal customers**

Internal customers are people who rely on you for information or to perform certain tasks so they can do their job. Basically, internal customers include just about everyone in your company, who work together to satisfy the expectations of external clients.

**Internal customer service providers**

Internal customer service providers are people you rely on to find or provide information, perform certain tasks, or help you in some way to perform your own tasks. You're their internal customer and you receive a service from them.

**External customers**

External customers are people you interact with over the phone, over the counter, or in your office, who don't belong to your organization. They're the ones who pay for your products or services, and keep your business running.

**Internal customer service relationships**

Unless you're right at the top of the customer service chain or only deal with external customers, you're probably both an internal customer and an internal service provider. You have some form of customer service relationship with most of your colleagues. So it's important to explore the nature of these relationships.

The first step to putting the whole customer service chain into perspective is to identify your internal customers. You should see yourself as providing a service to them.

Once you know who your internal customers are, you're in a better position to identify, explore, and satisfy their needs.

That way, you contribute to the overall quality of service your company provides to external customers, because you help the process run smoothly.

If you identify your internal customer service providers and pay attention to what they do for you, you develop a better idea of how the whole process works. You'll understand where information or tasks originate and what it takes to get them to you.

You also learn to recognize opportunities to help your internal service providers improve the service they provide to you.

**Question**

Why is it important to identify internal customer service relationships?

**Options:**

1. You develop a better understanding of the "big picture" and so find ways to add value to the customer service chain

2. You find it easier to meet the needs and expectations of internal customers

3. You can help your internal service providers to give you better service

4. You can identify problems with external customer service and find ways to improve

5. You develop a deeper understanding of the roles of others within an organization so you can do their jobs for them

**Answer:**

Option 1: This is a correct option. When you understand the details of how you and your colleagues interact, you'll be in a position to improve the overall process.

Option 2: This is a correct option. Once you know who your internal customers are, you'll be in a better position to improve your service to them.

Option 3: This option is correct. When you identify those colleagues who provide you with some form of internal service, you'll be in a position to make it easier for them to do so.

Option 4: This option is incorrect. Although external customer service might well be improved, this is an indirect result of identifying and improving your internal customer service relationships.

Option 5: This is an incorrect option. When you identify your internal customers and service providers, you take the first step to doing your own job better and to helping others do their jobs.

**How to identify internal dependencies**

Identifying your internal customer service relationships is easy. All you need to do is analyze the dependencies between you and your colleagues – either as individuals or as part of different teams or separate departments.

You can ask yourself "Who needs me to do my job so they can do theirs?" "Who do I provide services to?" "Who comes to me for information?" You probably interact with several people in many different ways.

Gloria works as a managing editor for a magazine. She has to liaise with authors of new submissions, the regular freelance writers, the editorial team, and the editor-in-chief before each new issue is released.

Follow along to find out how Gloria's colleagues interact with her.

**Editor-in-chief:** Curtis is the editor-in-chief, and Gloria's boss. He needs her to manage the daily administration of incoming submissions so when he comes to her for information, it's ready and waiting.

**Columnist:** Megan is a regular contributor with her own column. All articles have to be edited and typeset by a certain day each month, and Gloria's responsible for making sure that deadline's met. So Gloria needs Megan to hand in her articles on time.

**Writer:** Taku is a new writer who has just submitted an article for consideration. Gloria acts as a go-between for the editorial team and Taku to make sure Taku knows whether his contribution has been accepted for publication and what else is expected of him if it has been.

**Typesetter:** Rita heads the typesetting team. She needs Gloria to get articles to the editors so she can delegate typesetting work to her team. Then, she sends the final proofs to Gloria, who gives them to the editorial team.

Although she has no direct contact with the people who buy the magazine, Gloria interacts with a number of people – some rely on her, and she relies on others. If communication with colleagues like Curtis, Megan, Taku, and Rita were to break down, the publication process would be disrupted and the end product would be affected.

Select each colleague to learn more about why this person is Gloria's internal customer or internal customer service provider.

**Curtis**

Curtis relies on Gloria to keep a record of the status of things such as articles and deadlines. If Gloria doesn't do her job properly, he might receive misinformation, which could jeopardize the publication. So Gloria's work contributes to the quality of their end product and their authors' experience of the magazine.

Curtis is one of Gloria's internal customers. She provides a service to him that he relies on.

**Megan**

Gloria needs Megan to do her job so she can do her own. If Megan misses a deadline, Gloria won't get the article to the editorial team on time. In turn, that'll slow down the typesetting and printing processes and possibly delay the release of the magazine.

Megan provides an internal customer service to Gloria. Gloria needs certain information from Megan at specific times to do her own job.

**Taku**

Taku relies on Gloria to keep him updated about issues such as whether his article has been accepted, whether parts of it need to be rewritten, and when his final deadline is. He needs Gloria to give him this information in time so he can meet his own deadlines. If his experience of the magazine is bad, he might never write for it again.

Taku is one of Gloria's internal customers. She needs to provide him with timely information to help him do his job.

**Rita**

Rita needs Gloria to be up to speed about the articles to be included in the magazine so that Rita can meet her own deadlines. Similarly, Gloria needs Rita to be efficient so there's enough time to proofread the final pages. Otherwise, mistakes might creep into the magazine.

Rita is both an internal customer and an internal customer service provider for Gloria. At different stages of production, they both rely on each other to do certain tasks or provide information.

Gloria discovers who her internal customers are by searching for a dependency or inter-reliant relationship with a colleague. She identifies her internal customer service relationships by identifying which colleagues rely on her and which colleagues she relies on.

**Question**

Local municipalities send the Administration Department project proposals. Your department – the Finance Department – relays information to the Administration Department, which allocates resources to the local municipalities. You receive information from the Administration Department to compile budgets. You also provide local municipalities with their budgets and the mayor with financial statistics.

Match the players to their roles as internal customers or customer service providers to the Finance Department. Some players may be both.

**Options:**

A. Mayor
B. Administration Department
C. Local municipalities

**Targets:**

1. Internal customer
2. Internal customer service provider

**Answer:**

The mayor relies on you to keep her updated, the Administration Department relies on you for information, and the local municipalities rely on you to provide them with their yearly budgets.

The Administration Department provides you with information to compile your budgets and reports. You rely on its accuracy and timely delivery so you can perform your own duties properly.

**Understanding internal processes**

In a web, each strand is intricately connected. If one strand breaks, the whole structure may collapse. An organization is like a web. Each department, and each individual within that department, plays a part in supporting the overall structure.

It's important for different parts of a company to work together and understand each other's role in the organization. Companies that function well often realize this and encourage communication between different departments.

Some typical initiatives or activities companies use to foster this understanding include service level agreements, commonly known as SLAs, cross-functional steering groups, and service champions.

See each activity to find out what it involves.

**Service level agreements (SLAs)**

SLAs spell out what internal customers can reasonably expect from service providers. They're usually a formal document aimed at improving internal customer service and its terms are clear to everyone involved. SLAs ensure service expectations are communicated in advance, so service providers can manage their time and resources. Plus SLAs prevent animosity forming between internal customers and reduce the number of last-minute requests and unreasonable demands.

**Cross-functional steering groups**

Some organizations establish steering groups made of employees from various departments. Because a range of experiences from different levels of the organization are included, these groups are in a position to spearhead initiatives that improve internal communication and raise the level of internal customer service.

**Service champions**

Service champions are individuals who represent their departments or employees who perform the same function. They spearhead improvements by acting as go-betweens for management and their colleagues, and form unofficial links with other service champions. That way, a network of service champions is formed across the organization, which ensures a steady flow of communication between different departments and levels of management. Service champions often serve to motivate or influence their colleagues.

These initiatives improve internal customer service from an organizational perspective because they entrench systems that allow departments to communicate.

But no matter what initiatives, activities, or processes your company may have in place to facilitate interaction and communication between departments, as an individual you can do more to improve your relationship with colleagues you provide a service to.

A five-step process will help you deliver on your internal customers' needs. First, you list your internal customers. You get to know their work processes and roles in the organization. You discuss your mutual expectations openly. Then, you implement any action necessary to improve your internal customer service. Finally, you get feedback regularly, and evaluate and review the situation to keep the continuous improvement loop always open.

**Getting to know internal customers**

Unless you're completely self-employed and nobody relies on you to do their job, you interact with internal customers. Anyone who relies on you is an internal customer. Examples are a subcontracted company, another department within your company, or individuals within your department. Some of your colleagues may be both internal customers and internal service providers, meaning you have a mutually dependent relationship.

The first step to improving your internal customer service is to jot down a list of your internal customers. To do this, determine the relationships you have with different colleagues. Who needs your work to do their own job?

Once you've identified your internal customers, you should get to know their work processes and roles in the organization by gathering information about what they do and why they do it.

You can easily get this sort of perspective by chatting to colleagues from another part of your organization – take someone from another department to lunch or simply take a short break to interact with them.

While you talk, try to get an overall idea of how your roles function together. How does your work affect the big picture?

When you understand what a typical day involves for your internal customers, you'll know what you need to do to make their jobs easier, and you'll be more understanding about what it takes for them to get information or services to you when you need it.

Plus you'll develop an accurate mental picture of how different roles in the organization interact to create the final product. You'll have a better idea of your own place in this chain, and understand what you can do to improve the standard of the services you offer your colleagues.

For example, you're required to give Julia, from the HR Department, all requests for leave at least two months in advance. You find this frustrating because you struggle to plan that far ahead. But once you get to know Julia, you realize how stressful she finds the process of coordinating employee leave periods. After that, you try harder to submit your requests on time, and are happy to do so.

Clear communication between you and your internal customers is vital and will avoid disappointment due to miscommunication, misunderstandings, or lack of understanding. So it's important to talk openly to your colleagues about what you can expect from each other.

**Identifying mutual expectations**

If you and your internal customer understand the bigger picture and how you both fit into it, you have common ground from which to discuss your mutual expectations openly.

You should be frank about what can reasonably be expected from you. The internal customer service you provide still needs to align with your organization's goals and priorities.

For example, you work for an IT Department and one of your colleagues is fond of downloading role- playing games, although it's company policy to only use approved software. By removing the games

from his computer, you risk displeasing your internal customer. But if you don't do so, you'll take part in harming the company because you're not conserving bandwidth and are helping colleagues waste company time.

In this case, the needs of the company take priority over the needs of your internal customer. The "customer is always right" rule doesn't apply when satisfying your internal customers.

Of course, sometimes you might want to do an internal customer a favor. But this should be an exception rather than the rule or your internal customers will learn to expect the unreasonable of you.

You can avoid misunderstandings or animosity between you and your colleagues by following some simple guidelines:
- explain to your colleagues how they can be good customers – let them know what you need from them in order to meet their requests,
- openly discuss whether your internal customers' expectations are reasonable in terms of time and quality levels,
- know your customers' expectations of you – make sure you have all the information you need to fulfill a request, and
- be part of setting those expectations – if your customers' expectations are unrealistic, let them know.

For example, your boss expects you to present a proposal to your company's executive board. You make sure to find out exactly what she expects you to do so you won't disappoint her.

She asks you to print out documents comparing sales performances from the previous quarter with the current one so the board has ready access to the information during the presentation. This is a reasonable request and you agree.

But when she asks you to come up with estimates for the following quarter as well, you explain this is outside your realm of expertise. You agree to find someone else to compile this information.

**Question**

Gareth manages the call center of a delivery service company. His department and the dispatching and packaging departments don't get along. As a result, his company has a high staff turnover.

He's decided to try to improve the quality of internal customer service and has made a list of the people in other departments who rely on him for information.

What should he do next?

**Options:**

1. Get to know his internal customers and what a typical day involves for them

2. Discuss both his and his internal customers' expectations openly

3. Compile a list of all his internal customers

4. Set aside his own work processes to concentrate more fully on improving his internal customer service

**Answer:**

Option 1: This is a correct option. Gareth should first get to know the work processes and timelines of people in other departments so he understands what he can do to make their jobs easier. The best way to do this is simply to talk to them.

Option 2: This option is correct. Once Gareth understands what the other departments do, he'll be in a position to understand what's expected of him and what he can expect from others.

Option 3: This option is incorrect. Gareth's already identified his internal customers. Now he needs to get to know what their jobs entail and discuss their mutual expectations.

Option 4: This option is incorrect. Gareth should get to know his internal customers and talk to them about their mutual expectations. But these shouldn't interfere with his usual work.

**Taking action and getting feedback**

Once you've discussed your mutual expectations, you implement any action you think is necessary to meet the needs of your internal customers.

Again, you shouldn't have to take any action which takes up unreasonable amounts of your time, results in other internal customer needs being sidelined, or frustrates your organization's goals.

**Question**

You've probably worked with colleagues who act as if they think everyone else sits around doing nothing all day. When these people need something, they demand to have it immediately.

Why do you think this sort of behavior is counterproductive?

**Options:**

1. It results in a low level of service quality

2. It results in resentment on the part of the service provider

3. The internal customer acquires a reputation for being unreasonable or unprofessional

4. It slows up the production chain

**Answer:**

Option 1: This is a correct option. If you rush to get something to a customer, it won't be done as efficiently as when you plan to deliver the service and are able to manage your time.

Option 2: This is a correct option. When colleagues expect you to rush to their aid when they have a crisis, it becomes stressful. But when you know what's expected of you in advance, you'll be happy to provide that service.

Option 3: This is a correct option. If you and your internal customer have reasonable expectation of each other, you avoid the strain of constant surprises from colleagues who make unreasonable demands of you.

Option 4: This is an incorrect option. When people make last-minute demands it won't necessarily mean the service you provide will take longer. But the service you provide might be of lesser quality and will be more stressful to provide.

So when you write summaries for your colleague, you should make sure they're what he had in mind and suit his needs. Otherwise you need to come up with another solution.

**Question**

You manage the sales department at a company that manufactures kitchen appliances.

After speaking to various internal customers, you've decided you should relay comments you receive from external customers back to the design and manufacturing team. This would go a long way to fixing design flaws with the products, and involves minimal effort on your part compared to the improvements it would make.

What should you do next?

**Options:**

1. Implement a system where such information is given to the internal customers

2. Get feedback periodically from your internal customers to find out what else can be improved

3. Openly discuss the various ways you can improve your service delivery to your internal customers

4. Spend less time on your meetings with external customers in order to focus on your internal service delivery

**Answer:**

Option 1: This is a correct option. Once you have openly discussed how you can improve the service you provide to your internal customers, you should take any reasonable action. This is the next step in the process.

Option 2: This option is correct. Not only should you ensure the new system is working, but you should always be on the lookout for other ways to improve your internal customer service.

Option 3: This option is incorrect. If you and your internal customers have agreed on what needs to be done to improve your internal service delivery, this step has already taken place.

Option 4: This option is incorrect. As with the expectations you and your internal customers have of each other, any actions you take to improve the internal services you provide should not conflict with your organization's goals.

**Applying the process**

Stephanie is an advertising copywriter. Lately she's been getting a lot of negative feedback from the head of her department about some of her projects, partly because of frequent miscommunication between her and her colleagues. She decides it's time to improve her internal customer service to rectify the situation.

First Stephanie analyzes her work relationships so as to identify her internal customers. She writes down a list of people who rely on the output of her work.

She lists people such as Hans, her copy editor, the typesetter Janet, and Frankie, the designer. All three colleagues need her to complete her work on time so they can meet their own deadlines. At the same time, Stephanie needs them to do their jobs properly because their work affects the quality of the final product. And this in turn reflects on her abilities.

She also remembers to include Michaela, a researcher, who provides Stephanie with the information she needs to write her copy.

Next Stephanie tries to get to know what day-to-day life is like for her colleagues. She invites Hans, Janet, Frankie, and Michaela to spend lunchtime with her in the cafeteria so they can talk about their latest project and get a better idea of how their jobs interact.

See each colleague to learn more about this person's job.

### Stephanie

When Stephanie gets an assignment, she writes the copy according to the house style and project-specific guidelines. She relies on the research to provide details she'd otherwise spend a lot of time and effort searching for, such as prices and product history. Once she's written the copy, she sends it to her editor.

### Hans

Hans edits the copy for a number of projects and most days are very busy for him. He has to meet a number of deadlines and so it's important to him that Stephanie hands her work in on time. If she's running late, he needs to know in advance so he can rearrange his schedule. In the past, Stephanie's just given him her work as she finishes it, without regard for his schedule.

### Janet

Janet works in the Typesetting Department. She doesn't interact directly with Stephanie, but she relies on the copy and illustrations to be delivered to her on schedule or she fears she won't make her deadlines.

### Frankie

Once Stephanie's copy is edited, it goes to a designer like Frankie to illustrate the text. Frankie has his own deadlines and work processes that function alongside but separately from Stephanie's department. Often, there's little or no interaction between members of their departments, which causes errors and creates animosity between employees.

**Michaela**

Michaela works for the Research Department. Colleagues in this department interact with external customers to find out what sort of product they want and their target market. Stephanie relies on her to provide accurate and timely information.

As Stephanie talks to her colleagues, she develops a more holistic mental picture of the way their respective roles function together to create the end product. She also understands how her work affects other people.

Now she and her internal customers need to talk openly and honestly about their mutual expectations.

Follow along to find out what expectations Stephanie's colleagues have.

**Editor:** Hans asks her to deliver copy to editing on time. If she's running late, she should let him know so he can reorganize his own schedule. This is a reasonable request and won't take much effort on Stephanie's behalf.

**Typesetter:** Janet receives the illustrations and copy for typesetting at the same time. They often arrive after Stephanie's moved on to her next assignment. She says it would make her job easier if Stephanie is available to answer questions and oversee the typesetting process. But they agree that this falls outside Stephanie's job description.

**Designer:** Frankie needs to have more interaction with Stephanie to produce illustrations more closely aligned with what she had in mind when she wrote the copy. They agree a little more communication will go a long way to improve the quality of their work.

**Researcher:** Stephanie tells Michaela how much she relies on Michaela's research being accurate, thorough, and delivered on time. Michaela suggests Stephanie contacts her if she needs additional information.

Now Stephanie needs to implement any actions necessary to improve her internal customer service.

Hans and Michaela's expectations are easy to fulfill. By letting Hans know when she's running late and giving feedback to Michaela, she ensures the overall process is more efficient.

Janet and Frankie's requests will take more effort. Stephanie and Janet agree to talk to management about ways to integrate their departments. In Frankie's case, Stephanie agrees the extra effort is worth it because it'll improve the quality of the end product considerably.

Finally, Stephanie checks whether her actions are successful. This is an ongoing process – she should continuously seek out new ways to improve her internal customer service.

Stephanie starts by meeting with everyone once the first project is completed. She gets feedback to find out whether the process is smoother for everyone and where there's room for improvement.

Then, when she gets her next assignment, she repeats the process with her new internal customers.

Stephanie identified all the people who she relied on and who relied on her as her internal customers. By getting to know them and their work processes, she developed a clearer idea of how she fits into the system.

From this common ground, she and her colleagues were in a better position to openly discuss their expectations of each other and could discuss ways for Stephanie to improve her internal customer service.

Finally, Stephanie realized the sort of improvement she was after is an ongoing process. She resolved to keep finding ways to polish her interactions with her colleagues.

**The internal customer service attitude**

Natalie's house has been robbed. During this stressful time, the last thing she needs is for her insurance company to treat her badly. But when she calls them to find out about the status of her claim, the person she talks to says "It's not my job to help you. Someone will get hold of you later." She waits all day but nobody calls her back.

Joe, who should have taken Natalie's call, had to leave for a dentist's appointment so he asked a colleague to answer his phone while he was out. This colleague resented being asked to do something outside of her job description and, as a result, was quite rude over the phone to Natalie. Then she forgot to tell Joe about the call.

Because Joe's colleague had no interest in helping him out, Natalie's experience as a customer was negatively affected.

You've probably had a similar experience to Natalie at some time or another. Because the company you deal with is internally disorganized, you – the customer – have to take on the responsibility of extracting service from the organization.

Poor internal customer service – when people within an organization fail to help each other do their jobs – inevitably results in the external customer having a bad experience of the company.

To develop good internal customer service, the first thing you do is to develop the right attitude.

To develop an internal customer service attitude, you have to do three things. First you learn to see yourself as a service provider. You need to use common courtesy when dealing with your internal customers. And finally, you search for opportunities to exceed your internal customers' expectations.

**Being a service provider**

Companies tend to put a lot of emphasis on providing outstanding external customer service. To provide this service, a lot needs to be done behind the scenes. Often there's a higher number of interactions between people within an organization than of interactions with external customers.

**Question**

What do you think is the most important kind of customer service for companies to focus on?

**Options:**

1. Internal customer service
2. External customer service
3. Both – they're equally important

**Answer:**

Companies must focus on both internal and external customer service.

Option 1: Internal customer service is as important as external customer service. Arguably, it may even be more so if the company has complex internal relationships.

Option 2: You may find that putting all your efforts into improving external customer service will be ineffective if you ignore internal relationships. Employees within an organization have to function well together for its output to be of a good standard.

Option 3: It's true that having both good internal and external customer service is essential for a well- running company. This is because they're intimately connected – poor internal relationships will be reflected in the company's output.

The kind of relationship that exists between service providers and customers exists both within and outside of an organization. So for a business to run smoothly, you should give internal customer service as much attention as external customer service.

Keeping this in mind will help you put the whole process into perspective. When you learn to see your colleagues as customers and yourself as a service provider, you'll be able to help your colleagues and yourself to function well together.

In some organizations the relationship between internal customers and internal customer service providers is simple. For example, in a restaurant a waiter takes a customer's order, then gives it to the chef. The chef relies on the waiter to get the correct order so that he can do his job properly.

Other internal relationships might be more complex, where various colleagues or even whole departments rely on or serve each other.

## Customer Service Fundamentals

But no matter what the particulars are, all internal service ultimately affects the organization's external service.

All too often, people resent being asked to stop what they're doing to help colleagues. They see these requests as interruptions to their own success paths.

But if you take pride in your role as service provider, you learn to see a request or unusual demand as a chance to help your colleagues and improve their experience of the service you provide.

In turn, your colleagues will be far more willing to help you and so you'll find it easier to get your own work done.

**Question**

How does seeing yourself as a service provider help you to develop an internal customer service mentality?

**Options:**

1. It creates an atmosphere where people are willing to help each other

2. It allows you to understand the end experience of your external customers 3. It helps you understand what your internal customers need from you

**Answer:**

Option 1: This is the correct option. When you help others, they're more willing to help you. In turn, you and your colleagues will find it easier to do your jobs.

Option 2: This is an incorrect option. Seeing yourself as an internal customer service provider shouldn't affect the way you view your external customers, although it will indirectly improve external service.

Option 3: This option is incorrect. Knowing what your internal customers expect from you doesn't mean you'll try harder to fulfill those expectations.

**Using common courtesy**

The second thing you can do to develop an internal customer service attitude is to use common courtesy. Using simple words like "please" and "thank you" goes a long way to foster a healthy atmosphere in the workplace. By being polite, you keep your colleagues motivated, build rapport with them, and create a culture of sharing and helping.

See each benefit of being courteous for more information about it.

Keep your colleagues motivated

Even if you're just doing your job, it's always nice to feel appreciated. Hearing a heartfelt "thank you" when people provide information or perform a task they would have done anyway makes them feel better about doing that task. It keeps them motivated to do a good job.

**Build rapport**

Rather than treating your colleagues as cogs in a machine, or as means to your own ends, you should show your appreciation of what they do for you. If you show them you don't take them for granted, they'll feel better about themselves and their relationship with you. That way you add a human touch to your workplace relationships and create the basis for building rapport.

**Create a culture of sharing and helping**

By showing your appreciation of what others do for you, you foster a culture of sharing and helping in the workplace, which is essential for an internal customer service attitude. When people feel they have done something good, they feel better about themselves and their jobs – and so are more likely to want to help you again in the future.

You can show your appreciation of others in a number of ways. For example, you can show delight when you get a report from someone before the deadline.

You can explain how much someone's doing a small task for you has made your job so much easier that day.

Or you can express your gratitude when someone exceeds your expectations.

**Question**

In what ways does saying "please" and "thank you" help to create an internal customer service environment?

**Options:**

1. It encourages coworkers to assist each other

2. It helps build strong work relationships

3. It allows you to take pride in your interactions with others in the workplace

4. It allows you to focus on doing your job, which in turn benefits your internal customers

**Answer:**

Option 1: This is a correct option. Showing your appreciation of the work others do makes them feel better about themselves and creates a healthy atmosphere of sharing and helping.

Option 2: This option is correct. By using common courtesy, you build rapport and add a human touch to your relationships, which strengthens and enriches your interactions with others in the workplace.

Option 3: This is an incorrect option. By using common courtesy, you make others feel better about doing their jobs and about helping you.

Option 4: This option is incorrect. Saying "please" and "thank you" to others encourages others to feel motivated, rather than motivating yourself.

**Exceeding expectations**

Another thing you can do to develop your internal customer service attitude is to look for opportunities to exceed your internal customers' expectations of you.

When Natalie called her insurance company, imagine how surprised and delighted she would have been to receive excellent, polite customer service.

Your internal customers will be just as delighted if you exceed their expectations. Although it may not be possible every time, you should always be on the lookout for chances to go the extra mile for them.

Again, they'll be more willing to do the same for you in future. So you can help develop an atmosphere where people are willing to help each other do their jobs.

This could be as simple as handing in your daily reports a few hours before the end of the day. Or, if a colleague asked you for some information, you could surprise them by giving that person thorough research.

But remember exceeding expectations shouldn't be a distraction from your daily tasks or conflict with your organization's goals. Similarly, you shouldn't go the extra mile for one customer if it means cutting corners with your service for someone else.

**Question 1 of 2**

There is a lot of antagonism between various people at the factory Mary works at.

What should she do to develop an internal customer service attitude?

**Options:**

1. Accept that internal customers are as important as external customers

2. See herself as someone who provides services to her colleagues

3. Interpret work-related interruptions as a chance to improve her colleagues' experience of working with her

4. Keep in mind external customers are always more important than internal customers

5. Strike bargains with colleagues so when they do things for her, she'll help them in return

**Answer:**

Option 1: This is a correct option. Simply learning to see her colleagues as a type of customer will go a long way to improving the internal service Mary provides them.

Option 2: This option is correct. Mary should approach her interactions with colleagues as if she's providing a service to them.

Option 3: This is a correct option. If Mary interprets requests from colleagues as a chance to do something to help them, rather than as a nuisance, she'll be more polite and willing to help.

Option 4: This is an incorrect option. Because poor internal service can negatively affect the service external customers receive, Mary should accept her internal customer service relationships are just as important as those with external customers.

Option 5: This option is incorrect. If Mary always searches for opportunities to help her colleagues and make their jobs easier, she'll find it easy to be a good internal service provider.

**Question 2 of 2**

Which are examples of actions that demonstrate an internal customer service attitude?

**Options:**

1. Thanking a colleague when she provides you with information, even though it was her job to do so

2. Showing joy when someone does a small task that makes your job easier that day

3. Being on the lookout for ways to help your colleagues do their jobs

4. Thanking a colleague only when he goes beyond the call of duty to help you out 5. Bending the rules so you can exceed your colleagues' expectations of you

**Answer:**

Option 1: This is a correct option. Using common courtesy makes your interactions with your colleagues more human and greatly improves internal customer service.

Option 2: This option is correct. Showing your colleagues how much you appreciate their work makes them feel better about their job and improves your relationships with them.

Option 3: This is a correct option. If you always try to improve your internal service, you'll often spot easy ways to make your colleagues' jobs easier.

Option 4: This option is incorrect. You should use common courtesy all the time, even when your colleagues are just doing their jobs. That way they'll feel better about themselves and your relationship will improve.

Option 5: This is an incorrect option. While you should try to exceed your internal customers' expectations, doing so will be counterproductive if it interferes with your company's goals.

# CHAPTER THREE
*Customer Service in the Field*

**Stages of on-site customer service**

Suzanne visits her customers on a regular basis to get feedback on her company's products, and John, who's a sales representative, often goes on locations to promote his products. Mary's job involves repairing computers, so she frequently visits clients at their homes or offices.

To provide a satisfactory level of customer service, Suzanne, John, and Mary follow specific guidelines. They consider visiting customers as a process with five stages, including preparation, arrival, service, wrap up, and follow up.

The first stage – preparation – is an important one. If you don't prepare properly before arriving at a customer's business or home, it's likely you'll make a poor impression. You might also end up simply wasting the customer's time.

To prepare appropriately for visiting a customer, you need to explain or clarify the reason for a proposed visit and set a mutually convenient meeting time. You should

## Customer Service Fundamentals

then gather as much relevant information as you can about the customer.

See each guideline for preparing for a customer visit for more information about it.

**Clarify the reason for a visit**

You may be notified of a customer's request for a visit – for example, via telephone, e-mail, fax, or your organization's electronic logging system. You should then take note of the reason for the request, asking for further clarification if necessary, and acknowledge your receipt of it.

Alternatively, you may be the one who initiates a visit. In this case, it's important that when you contact the customer, you clearly explain your reason for proposing a visit.

**Set a mutually convenient meeting time**

It's important you set a time and date for the visit that won't inconvenience the customer, and that you'll be able to stick to. You should make it clear that you respect the value of the customer's time.

**Gather information about the customer**

You should gather relevant information about the customer and about the problem or issue you need to address during a visit. As well as ensuring you'll be better prepared to serve the customer during a visit, knowing something about the customer can help you personalize the service you provide.

Customers appreciate being recognized. They're likely to feel more valued if you're familiar with the details of their accounts, show an interest in them, and have an understanding of their business concerns. Proper research before visits – for example, using your organization's client database – can equip you to relate better to customers and their needs.

Once you've prepared adequately for your appointment with a customer, you're set for the second stage of the on-site customer service process – arrival.

Be conscious that when you arrive, you set the tone for the rest of the visit, and your demeanor determines how the client reacts to you. So at this point, it's especially important to come across as professional, friendly, helpful, and approachable.

It's also important to dress appropriately, depending on the reason for a visit. For example, a business suit is probably best if you're a sales representative. Clean overalls are more appropriate if you need to inspect a customer's roof or replace a car part.

In any situation, though, ensuring you're well groomed is a basic step in making a good first impression on a customer.

When you first arrive at a customer's home or business, it's important you start by identifying yourself clearly and reminding the customer of the reason for your visit. You should have established and clarified this with the customer during the preparation phase.

You should also set expectations. If you need to complete a job, for instance, specify approximately how long the job will take and what you need to do.

After introducing yourself, you can help set the right tone by starting off a visit with some small talk. Also, it's important to practice customer recognition – that is, to show you recognize the customer's individuality and specific needs.

See each tip to learn more about it.

## Customer Service Fundamentals

**Start with small talk**

Small talk is useful for breaking the ice and can help you set the tone for your visit. Be sure though to choose appropriate topics for small talk.

You could talk about the weather, entertainment news, or current events, but steer clear of controversial, personal, or negative comments. You need to remain professional at all times, including in the choice of subject matter you discuss with customers.

**Practice customer recognition**

Using information you gather during the preparation stage, you can set a good tone for a visit by demonstrating that you're familiar with the customer and her needs.

Always remember that your customer is an individual. Simply addressing her by name or referring briefly to her line of business can make her feel more comfortable and valued.

Additional tips to bear in mind during the arrival stage are to make good eye contact – as a way to acknowledge the customer – and to practice active listening. Poor listening leads to misunderstandings, which in turn lead to bad service. When you listen actively, you give the customer your full attention, demonstrate that you understand what he's saying, and if you're not sure, ask him to explain.

Once you've made a good first impression and have established expectations, the core stage of your visit to a customer can occur – that of providing the required service.

If you're a technician out on a service call, this is the stage at which you'll complete the necessary repair, installation, or other service work. And if you're a sales representative, this is when you'll deliver your sales pitch.

In some cases, it's clear what service you must provide and how. For example, you may need simply to deliver a part to a customer and obtain this person's signature. Often though, providing appropriate service involves performing four steps:

- evaluate the situation you have to deal with – for example, determining exactly how a customer's printer is malfunctioning,
- validate your understanding of the job and what it entails – for instance, by confirming the problem and the required outcome with the customer,
- decide on what it is you need to do – such as fixing a printer that overheats, and
- develop and execute a plan of action – for example, a plan that outlines when and who will replace the broken printer component and test its functionality.

Throughout the service stage, it's critical to continue communicating well with the customer. This requires good active listening skills on your part, or you may miss important information or concerns.

It also requires that you keep the customer fully informed. Remember three simple things – tell the customer what you're planning to do, what you're doing, and then what it is you've done.

When you're talking about the plan of action you're following or the work you're doing, it's important you take the customer's level of knowledge into account. You should avoid jargon and technical terminology the customer is unlikely to be familiar with. Rather than impressing a customer, this is likely to leave him confused and dissatisfied.

Once you've completed the service stage, you move into the wrap-up stage. During this stage, you apply these golden rules:

- tidy up the area you've worked in, clearing it of any mess or items you've used,
- confirm and demonstrate what you've installed or repaired is working,
- summarize issues or key points arising from the service,
- ask questions to confirm the customer is satisfied with the service,
- escalate any issues if necessary, and answer any customer queries that arise.

See each rule you should apply during the wrap-up stage to learn more about it.

### Tidy up

It's disrespectful and creates a poor impression with customers if you leave a mess behind you. Tidying up may involve clearing any debris or dust, and packing away or returning items you've used. If you were offered coffee, for example, you may want to return the cup to the customer's kitchen.

To leave the customer with a positive impression, make sure you leave the premises exactly as you found them when you arrived.

### Confirm and demonstrate

If you've installed or repaired something, it's important you test that it is in fact working before you leave the customer's premises. A customer who discovers that a problem hasn't been fixed only after you leave is likely to be frustrated and annoyed, and will have to waste time calling your company back to arrange a second visit.

**Summarize**

In the wrap-up phase, you should summarize – or reaffirm – the main points or issues that have come out of your visit with the customer. This is part of the active listening process – it serves to ensure you've understood your client and the client has understood you.

When relevant, you should also summarize any necessary or agreed steps for following up on a customer's problem.

**Ask questions**

Once you've completed your job, you should confirm whether the customer is satisfied with the service you provided. Your company may provide you with standard questions to ask the customer at this point – or you may simply ask if the customer is satisfied.

**Escalate issues**

Not all installations, repairs, or visits to customers are successful, and sometimes it's necessary to refer issues to other departments or individuals within your company.

If this occurs, assure the customer you're escalating the matter and will keep her informed about how it'll be resolved.

**Answer queries**

Part of the wrap-up process is giving the customer the opportunity to ask questions. You should ask if the customer has any queries before you leave, even if you answered various questions during the service phase.

The last stage of the on-site customer service process is the follow-up phase. You may need to follow up if you've

## Customer Service Fundamentals

had to escalate an issue or if the customer requests a service other than the one you provided during a visit.

In these cases, you should take ownership of the follow-up process – ensure the customer can deal with you directly. You don't want the customer to repeat all the details of a situation to new and unfamiliar staff within your company.

You may also follow up on a visit simply to ensure the customer is satisfied. For example, questions you might ask in a follow-up call are "Is everything OK?" "Are things still in working order?" "Are you experiencing any more problems?" and "Do you have any other queries?" This is an opportunity to address any remaining problems and to show the customer that you're dedicated to providing high-quality service.

**Question**

You need to visit a customer's home to replace a faulty hot water tank your company originally installed.

Match the stages of the on-site customer service process to corresponding examples of actions you should take.

**Options:**

A. Follow up
B. Service
C. Arrival
D. Preparation
E. Wrap up

**Targets:**

1. Contact the customer to ask if the replacement tank you installed is working properly
2. Listen to the customer's concerns and explain what you're doing clearly as you replace the faulty tank

3. Say you've come to replace the tank and then break the ice by commenting on traffic conditions in town

4. Establish a suitable time for replacing the tank and review details of the customer's account 5. Summarize what's occurred and ask if the customer has any additional queries

**Answer:**

During the follow-up stage, you take any further steps required to resolve a customer's problem or simply call back to ensure that all is in order.

During the service stage, you complete the work or provide the service that's required. In this stage, it's important to listen actively and communicate clearly with the customer.

During the arrival stage, you should remind the customer of the purpose of your visit. It's also a good idea to use small talk to put the customer at ease and set a good tone for the visit.

During the preparation stage, you need to clarify the reason for a visit, set a mutually convenient meeting time, and gather relevant background information about the customer's account.

During the wrap-up stage, you should summarize what has occurred during the visit and any required follow-up steps. Before leaving, you should also give the customer an opportunity to ask any remaining questions.

**Introduction to service on site**

Visiting a customer's home or business premises to provide a service can be challenging. It requires you to adapt to a new environment. And because you interact face-to-face with the customer, your interpersonal skills are put to the test. Using a range of strategies, though, will help ensure you always leave customers impressed with the quality of the service you provided.

To provide excellent customer service on site, you apply four main strategies:
- start on a positive note to set the right tone for the rest of the visit,
- set expectations clearly to avoid getting sidetracked or disappointing the customer,
- listen actively to make sure you understand everything the customer wants, and
- help customers understand your products or service so they recognize the benefits.

See each strategy for more information on how to apply it.

**Start on a positive note**

You set the tone for the whole visit on a positive note if you start your interaction with the customer correctly. You should say something to break the ice. Communication will be easier and the customer is more likely to be satisfied with the service you provide.

**Set expectations clearly**

Setting your customer's expectations is an important step to ensure customer satisfaction. By letting your customer know what you're there to do, roughly how long it'll take, and the length of time any further services may take, you make sure you both understand each other.

**Listen actively**

Active listening is always a vital element in providing effective customer service. It's a strategy for ensuring you fully understand your customer. It also demonstrates that you care about what the customer has to say.

**Help customers understand your product or services**

An on-site visit provides a perfect opportunity for you to explain your company's product and its proper use – or your company's services – to a customer. Often, customers feel more free to ask a question in person than on the telephone. Also, because you're with the customer in person, you may be able to demonstrate how to use or set up a product

**Starting on a positive note**

Often, how well you connect with a customer depends on the way you start a visit. First impressions are important and can set the tone for the rest of your visit. If you take care to make a customer feel comfortable and to project a professional image at this point, your interactions are far more likely to yield positive results.

You should make sure you arrive at a customer's home or place of business punctually, at the agreed time.

To make a good impression, you also need to prepare properly for the visit. You should arrive with all relevant information and tools at hand, and know what's required. An administrative hiccup at the outset can make a lasting, negative impression.

Breaking the ice is the first step in starting things off on the right foot. To do this, you can offer a warm greeting, practice customer recognition, and use small talk to get the ball rolling.

See each technique for more information about breaking the ice.

**Offer a warm greeting**

Offer a warm greeting to demonstrate warmth and a personal touch. By showing a personal interest in your customer, you'll establish rapport.

**Practice customer recognition**

Practice customer recognition to make the customer feel valued. Demonstrate, for example, that you know his name, buying habits, and what product or service he bought last from your company.

**Use small talk**

Use small talk to get things started and establish an easy flow of conversation. However, avoid controversial topics like religion or politics, or overly personal comments.

As well as using other techniques for breaking the ice, you should project a sense of easy professionalism with your body language. If you maintain an open posture, make eye contact, and actively show interest, you'll succeed in making a connection with your customer.

Also, nonverbal signals, like nodding and smiling at the appropriate times, will reassure the customer that you're listening and understanding what they're saying.

**Question**

What are examples of ways you can start a visit to a customer on a positive note?

**Options:**

1. Open with a friendly greeting that invites a response
2. Immediately begin the work you need to complete during the visit, recognizing that your customer's time is valuable

3. Use the customer's name and demonstrate familiarity with this person's line of business or previous interactions with your company

4. Chat briefly about an issue that's not controversial – like pretty scenery surrounding the client's home or office

5. Maintain a highly formal demeanor

**Answer:**

Option 1: This is a correct option. Adding a personal touch to your greeting will help you break the ice and connect with the customer on a personal level.

Option 2: This option is incorrect. It's generally good practice to establish a personal connection with a customer before you begin providing the service that's the reason for your visit. This helps ensure better communication throughout the visit, as well as demonstrating that you respect and value the customer.

Option 3: This is a correct option. It's important to demonstrate that you recognize the customer as an individual. Also, showing that you're familiar with this person's history with your company or line of business demonstrates that you value the customer, and makes it easier to establish a personal connection.

Option 4: This is a correct option. Engaging in small talk is a good way to break the ice and establish rapport with a customer.

Option 5: This option is incorrect. Although a highly formal demeanor might appear professional, people generally respond better to those who take the time to get to know them and demonstrate a degree of care about them on a personal level.

**Setting expectations clearly**

To avoid disappointing customers during service calls, you need to set their expectations clearly. You should be up front in specifying exactly what you'll be doing and, as far as possible, how long this will take. Otherwise customers may have expectations you'll fail to meet.

The best policy to follow when letting customers know what to expect is to be honest. For example, be as accurate and realistic as possible – and if factors beyond your control affect the time it takes to complete a job, say so.

You'll be seen as professional and reliable if you deliver on exactly what you've said, whereas a glib promise accompanied by a late delivery can create a lasting negative impression.

Also, making it clear what you can and cannot do during a service call can prevent you from leaving a customer unsatisfied.

## Customer Service Fundamentals

Say you need to visit a customer who's setting up an office network so that you can finalize the sale of several new computers. During the visit, the customer expects you to be able to fix a technical networking problem. You can't assist, so the customer is disappointed. Inconveniences like these usually won't happen if you set realistic expectations about your visit beforehand.

**Question**

Which examples of pitfalls can you avoid by clearly setting a customer's expectations about an on-site visit?

**Options:**

1. A customer becoming upset because a job takes longer than expected

2. A customer being called away suddenly during your presentation

3. A customer asking you to perform a service for which you are unqualified but that relates to work done by your company

4. A customer finding your manner off-putting

**Answer:**

Option 1: This option is correct. Setting a customer's expectations involves making it clear how long a job will take to complete, as well as what the job will involve.

Option 2: This is an incorrect option. Setting a customer's expectations includes letting them know how long your visit will take, but can't prevent external factors beyond your control from disrupting a visit.

Option 3: This is a correct option. An important aspect of setting a customer's expectations is making it clear exactly what service you'll be able to provide during a visit.

Option 4: This option is incorrect. Adopting an appropriate and friendly manner during a visit is an important part of providing excellent customer service on site, but doesn't relate to setting clear expectations.

**Listening actively**

A general rule is that a poor listener will provide poor customer service. If you don't listen actively, you may fail to pick up on important information, and you won't appear to be focusing on the customer's needs and concerns.

Several active listening techniques can help you communicate well with customers. You should paraphrase and restate what a customer says, and look for nonverbal cues to help you understand how the customer feels. Do not attempt to speed up the conversation. And summarize the gist of what the customer has said and query their satisfaction.

See each technique for more information about it.

**Paraphrase and restate**

By paraphrasing or restating what a customer has said, you demonstrate you're paying attention. You also give the customer the opportunity to hear you've understood correctly.

You can introduce your rewording of what a customer has said using phrases like "Am I right in believing..." and "So you're telling me..."

**Look for nonverbal cues**

Nonverbal cues like body language and tone of voice can help you understand a customer's emotions when his words don't convey the whole message.

Often, showing you recognize how a customer is feeling can help you get to the heart of a matter. For example, starting a response with something like "You seem pleased with..." or "You sound very doubtful about..." encourages a customer to elaborate. It also shows you understand the customer and acknowledge his perspective.

**Don't speed up the conversation**

As an active listener, your role is to understand what your customer's telling you. One surefire way to sabotage this is by speeding up the conversation or jumping in with an opinion or solution before a customer has finished speaking. This shows you're thinking about your response while the customer's still speaking to you, rather than listening fully.

**Summarize and query satisfaction**

Once a customer finishes speaking, it's a good idea to summarize the gist of what he's said to ensure you've understood correctly and demonstrate you're paying close attention. You can begin doing this using phrases like "I understand your main concerns are..." and "To recap the important issues..."

Once you've done this and specified the actions you plan to take to address the customer's concerns, it's important to ask if the customer is satisfied with your proposal.

**Question**
What do you think the benefits of active listening are?
**Options:**
1. Makes customers feel as though you care about what they have to say
2. Helps you save time by anticipating what the customer has to say before she says it
3. Makes the customer more likely to listen to what you have to say in return for listening to him
4. Helps you establish a more personal rapport with the customer

**Answer:**
Option 1: This option is correct. Active listening can demonstrate that you care deeply about what the customer has to say.

Option 2: This is an incorrect option. If you practice active listening, you will take time to listen to everything the speaker says, and not try to save time by anticipating what she might say.

Option 3: This option is incorrect. There should be no expectation of a speaker returning the favor and listening to you. An active listener's job is to facilitate a productive exchange and take in information rather than just waiting to speak.

Option 4: This is a correct option. By demonstrating that you're really interested in what is being said, you'll make a personal connection with the customer.

Active listening has several benefits. It makes customers feel you care about what they have to say and reassures them that you'll take their input into account when determining what actions to take. It also enables you to establish a connection with customers so that productive communication occurs.

**Improving customer understanding**

Often, an on-site visit is the perfect opportunity to help a customer understand your company's products or services better. Customers feel more free to ask questions face-to-face than over the phone or in an e-mail. And taking the time to ensure they know how to get the most out of a product or service can result in better customer satisfaction.

When explaining your product or service to a customer, you need to do so in a friendly and professional manner. You should use simple language and avoid jargon, and – where possible – use some of the customer's own words in your explanation.

See each guideline to increase understanding for more information about it.

**Use simple language and avoid jargon**

It's important to explain a product or service in a way that's easy for the customer to understand. Accordingly, you should avoid technical or business jargon. This can cause confusion and alienate a customer who doesn't understand it.

**Use the customer's own words**

If possible, try explaining your product using some of your customer's vocabulary. Odds are that customers won't know all the trade-specific vocabulary for a specialist product, but they'll be able to grasp the gist of it if you use words and concepts they already understand.

**Examples of effective on-site service**

Jason is a florist who's preparing several floral arrangements for Susan, a client who's a wedding planner. Susan has been frustrated by a number of last-minute changes made by the couple, and has called Jason to her office, the day before the wedding.

Follow along as Jason visits Susan in her office on the day before the wedding.

*Jason:* Good morning Susan. How are things going?

*Susan:* Good morning, I'm doing OK, if slightly frazzled. I'm glad you're here because they've asked for more last-minute changes!

*Jason:* I see. How can I help?

*Susan:* The flower arrangements need slight tweaking if they're to fit with the new decorations.

*Jason:* OK, that shouldn't be much of a problem, and it's such a lovely day to be working on something like this.

*Susan:* I suppose it is. These last-minute changes always annoy me though. Jason: I'm sure things will work out, and there shouldn't be any problems from my side.

*Susan:* Thanks Jason. I know I can always rely on you.

**Question**

Which of Jason's statements and inquiries reflect the best practice of starting on a positive note by breaking the ice?

**Options:**

1. "Good morning Susan. How are things going?"
2. "I see. How can I help?"
3. "OK, that shouldn't be much of a problem."
4. "It's such a lovely day to be working on something like this."
5. "I'm sure things will work out, and there should be no problem from my side."

**Answer:**

Option 1: This is a correct option. Jason's warm greeting and use of Susan's name is a good way to break the ice. It demonstrates care for his customer on a personal level.

Option 2: This option is incorrect. This inquiry is entirely work related – it isn't part of an attempt to break the ice by establishing a personal connection with a customer.

Option 3: This is an incorrect option. This response relates specifically to Susan's work request – it isn't designed to help Jason establish a personal connection with his customer.

Option 4: This option is correct. By mentioning the weather, Jason helps break the ice. This is an example of using small talk to help establish a personal connection with a customer.

Option 5: This is an incorrect option. This sentence is entirely work related.

Next consider Joe, who is a very busy freelance architect. After a friend of his in the same line of work suffers a minor heart attack, Joe decides to get in shape. He calls Sarah, a personal trainer from the local gym, and arranges for her to visit him at home to advise him on a suitable exercise routine.

Follow along as Sarah meets Joe to discuss an exercise program with him.

**Sarah:** Hi Joe. It's nice to meet you. I'm Sarah – and I'll be helping you get in shape.

*Sarah is smiling.*

**Joe:** Hi Sarah, thanks for coming over. As I mentioned in my e-mail, I have a home gym and I'm not too sure what to do with it...

*Joe looks a little uncertain.*

**Sarah:** Super – so you have a home gym. We'll have you fit in no time! Sarah is smiling and energetic, and oblivious to what Joe wants.

**Joe:** Uh – I'd really like to start off gently, and then settle on a workout I can fit into my busy schedule so that...

*Joe looks slightly upset.*

**Sarah:** OK, so you have a busy schedule. But I'm sure we can fit in a session each morning and then before supper. We can focus on aerobic fitness and fit in some upper body strength exercises. Perhaps some running in the evenings.

*Sarah is smiling and energetic.*

**Joe:** I think perhaps that is too much to start with. Maybe I can show you the exercise room?
*Joe looks quizzical.*
**Sarah:** That'd be great. So we need to work out a program to suit your schedule.
Sarah looks pleased.
**Joe:** Yes, that's really what I want.

**Question**

Sarah didn't do a good job of listening to her customer, but she did manage to apply one of the active listening techniques.

Which technique does Sarah demonstrate during her conversation with Joe?

**Options:**
1. Paraphrase and restate
2. Look for nonverbal clues
3. Don't speed up the conversation
4. Summarize and query satisfaction

**Answer:**

Option 1: This is the correct option. Sarah rephrases components of each of Joe's statements to demonstrate that she's picked up and understands the points he made.

Option 2: This is an incorrect option. Sarah doesn't notice Joe's nervous expression or tone of voice, and doesn't adjust her responses accordingly.

Option 3: This option is incorrect. At one point Sarah actually cuts Joe off. She also responds to his statements immediately, without taking time to think of a plan of action that will suit his needs.

Option 4: This option is incorrect. Sarah doesn't inquire whether Joe is happy with her suggestions or with the way their conversation is progressing.

# CHAPTER FOUR
*Customer Service over the Phone*

**Basic telephone etiquette rules**

Wendy is having difficulty with software she just purchased. She calls the manufacturer's customer care line, hoping for a quick solution to the problem. After dialing the number, she waits for more than a minute – and starts to wonder if she dialed the correct number – before a customer service representative answers her call.

Follow along as Todd, a customer service representative, takes Wendy's call.

**Todd:** Hello. Todd speaking.

*Todd is relaxed.*

**Wendy:** Hi. Is this the Diallonic customer care center?

*Wendy is uncertain.*

**Todd:** Yup. What can I do for you?

*Todd asks.*

**Wendy:** I purchased your communications management suite, but I'm having trouble loading the e-mail module. It won't sync with my e-mail account.

*Wendy is concerned*

## Customer Service Fundamentals

**Todd:** Hold on. I'll be right back.
*Todd is distracted.*
**Todd:** OK, so what was your problem again?
*Todd asks.*
**Wendy:** The e-mail module. It won't sync with my e-mail account.
*Wendy is annoyed.*
**Todd:** Sounds tricky. You better speak to Mike. He knows more about that. Let me put you through.
*Todd is unconcerned.*
**Wendy:** Hello? Todd? Hello?
*Wendy is angry.*

Needless to say, Wendy wasn't satisfied with the way Todd handled her call. She contacted the customer care center hoping for assistance. Instead Todd failed to answer promptly or identify his company, and he didn't seem interested in resolving her query.

If Todd had applied a few simple strategies, he could have made a better impression on Wendy and left her feeling good about the call – even if he had to transfer her to another customer service representative who's better equipped to solve her problem.

But Todd failed to apply basic telephone etiquette rules. Instead, he upset the customer and came across as unprofessional.

### Question

What mistakes do you think Todd made in handling the call from Wendy?

Options:
1. He put her on hold in an abrupt manner
2. He didn't offer assistance to her
3. He took too long to answer her call

4. His greeting was too vague

5. He transferred her in a way that made her feel confident her query would be answered

**Answer:**

Although Todd came across as unprofessional, he did offer assistance – and it may have been necessary for him to pass the customer's problem to another service representative. His specific mistakes were making the customer wait too long before answering the call, failing to use the company's name or identify his department when he did, not asking the customer what her query was, and then seemingly abandoning her call, without any explanation.

Following basic rules of telephone etiquette can help you avoid the types of mistakes Todd made. It ensures you project a professional image over the phone and leave callers satisfied.

Specific rules of etiquette apply for answering a call, putting a customer on hold, transferring a call, and closing a call.

To answer a call correctly, it's important to start by answering it promptly – generally within three rings. A customer left waiting for longer than this may be annoyed at the delay and is unlikely to feel that your company prioritizes its customer service.

Next you should greet the customer and identify yourself and your company or department. It's important to do this before asking the customer for information such as a reference number – first the customer needs to know who she's talking to.

Finally, you should offer your assistance to the customer.

## Customer Service Fundamentals

As well as answering a call correctly, it's important to follow proper etiquette when you put customers on hold. Failing to do this can leave customers frustrated and confused about why their call isn't being dealt with. When it's necessary to put someone on hold, you should perform five key steps – ask for permission, explain, give an estimate of how long the customer will have to wait, provide an update if necessary, and thank the customer for holding.

See each step to find out more about it.

**1. Ask**

You should always ask if you can put the customer on hold. It's very important to get the customer's permission before doing so.

**2. Explain**

Explain why you're putting the customer on hold or what you'll do while the call is on hold.

**3. Estimate**

You give the customer an estimate of how long you'll put the call on hold so the customer knows what to expect and can make a decision about whether to remain on hold or end the call and try again later.

**4. Update**

If you need to keep the customer on hold for longer than expected, update the customer by explaining why you're taking so long and how much longer you think you need. If the customer can't wait, offer to call back at a later time.

**5. Thank**

When you're ready to resume the call, you thank the customer for being patient while on hold.

**Question**

Which actions should you take when putting customers on hold?

**Options:**

1. Inform customers you're going to put them on hold
2. Tell customer why you need to put them on hold
3. Give customers an idea of how long they'll be on hold
4. Show customers gratitude for their patience while on hold
5. Seek customers' permission before putting them on hold
6. Hang up if the hold is taking longer than expected
7. Inform customers if the hold's duration changes from the initial expectation

**Answer:**

Option 1: This is an incorrect option. You shouldn't tell customers you're putting them on hold – you should rather ask them if you can put them on hold.

Option 2: This option is correct. You should explain to customers why you're putting them on hold.

Option 3: This is a correct option. You should estimate the duration of the hold, so customers know what to expect.

Option 4: This option is correct. When you resume the call, you should thank customers for holding.

Option 5: This is a correct option. You should always ask if you may put customers on hold.

Option 6: This option is incorrect. You should never deliberately hang up on customers without prior warning.

Option 7: This option is correct. If the hold is taking longer than expected, you should give customers an update – explaining the reason for the delay and estimating how much longer the hold should take.

If you have to transfer a customer's calls to a colleague or another department, it's important to explain to the customer who you're transferring the call to and why, or how the person you're handing the call to will be able to help.

When possible, you should also speak to the person to whom you plan to transfer the call so that you can explain who the customer is and what the problem or query is.

This ensures customers don't have to repeat everything they've already told you to someone else. It's especially important if customers are likely to be transferred numerous times during a call.

To close a call appropriately, it's important to summarize and then check the customer's satisfaction, offer further assistance, thank the customer, and hang up only after the customer does.

See each step to find out how to accomplish it.

**1. Summarize and check satisfaction**

Remind the customer of any actions you've agreed to take to resolve the query and of any actions the customer may need to take. You should also ensure the customer understands and is satisfied with the way the query has been addressed.

**2. Offer further assistance**

You ask the customer if you can offer assistance with any other issues. This allows the customer to bring up any points that still need resolution or to make any new requests or queries.

**3. Thank the customer**

When closing the call, you always thank the customer and express appreciation. For example, you could thank the customer for informing you of a particular issue. This helps you to end the call on a positive note.

**4. Hang up**

You hang up the phone only after the customer has put down the phone. This prevents you from inadvertently cutting off the customer in mid-sentence.

Following these steps ensures you end the call positively, hopefully leaving the customer with a good impression of you and your company.

After ending a call, you need to record any important information – such as the details of the follow-up steps you've agreed to take – so you don't forget and you take the correct action.

Remember Todd, who made a poor impression on Wendy who called about a software problem? Follow along as he takes the same call from Wendy, but this time, he applies the basic rules of telephone etiquette.

**Todd:** Good morning, Diallonic Customer Care Center, Todd speaking. How may I help you?

*Todd says, professionally.*

**Wendy:** Hi Todd. I purchased your company's communications management suite, but I'm having trouble loading the e-mail module. It won't sync with my e-mail account.

*Wendy is uncertain.*

**Todd:** Could you please hold for about one minute? I need to access the product database so I can assist you.

**Todd asks, confidently.**

**Wendy:** Sure, no problem.

*Wendy agrees to Todd's request.*

**Todd:** Thanks so much for holding. My colleague, Mike, is an expert on the module. He'll be able to assist you much quicker than I can. Would you mind if I transfer you to him?

*Todd asks.*

**Wendy:** Um, yes – that's fine. Thanks so much for the help!

*Wendy is pleased.*

Todd applied the basic rules of etiquette for answering a call, putting the customer on hold, and transferring the call. As a result, he made a good impression on Wendy and left her satisfied with the service she received, even though he wasn't able to resolve her query himself.

**Question**

Why is it important to follow the basic rules of etiquette for handling telephone calls?

**Options:**

1. To prevent angry customers from verbally abusing you

2. To help you project a professional image

3. To ensure you always succeed in resolving customers' problems

**Answer:**

Option 1: This option is incorrect. Handling calls professionally is an important aspect of providing good customer service. However, customers who are upset or angry for any reason may become abusive during calls, even if you follow the basic rules of etiquette.

Option 2: This is the correct option. Following the basic rules of telephone etiquette ensures you provide professional and competent customer service.

Option 3: This is an incorrect option. You may not have the knowledge or resources to resolve specific customers' problems and sometimes it's necessary to transfer calls to others who are better equipped to handle them. It's important, though, to follow the basic etiquette rules for doing this.

**Question**

What are the basic rules of etiquette for handling telephone calls?

**Options:**

1. Begin a call by taking the customer's name and, if relevant, reference number
2. Specify how long a customer who agrees to be put on hold should expect to wait
3. Answer a call within three rings
4. Thank the customer when closing a call
5. Open a call by asking how you can help
6. Before transferring a call, explain the customer's query to the person you're forwarding the call to

**Answer:**

Option 1: This is an incorrect option. You should begin a call by greeting the customer, identifying yourself and your company or department, and then offering assistance. Once you've done this and given the caller a chance to respond, it may be appropriate to take down the customer's details before continuing.

Option 2: This is a correct option. Before putting a customer on hold, you should give an estimate of how long the customer will have to wait. The customer can then decide whether to remain on hold or end the call and try again later.

Option 3: This option is correct. To appear professional, it's important to answer customers' calls promptly.

Option 4: This is a correct option. Thanking the customer helps you to end a call on a positive note.

Option 5: This option is incorrect. You should answer a call by greeting the customer, identifying yourself and your company or department, and then offering assistance.

Option 6: This is a correct option. Ensuring that the person to whom you transfer a customer's call knows who the caller is and what the call is about means that the customer doesn't have to repeat what they've already told you.

**Minding your tone of voice**

You deliver excellent service if you care about the details. It's the little things that take over-the-phone customer service from average or good to exceptional.

Five strategies help you deliver outstanding customer service over the telephone. To excel, you need to mind your tone of voice, show you're listening, use customer-focused language, help resolve problems, and mirror your customer's language.

In a face-to-face conversation, meaning isn't carried by words alone – it's also conveyed through body language and tone of voice.

You don't transmit physical cues like facial expressions and posture over the phone. However, your tone of voice conveys your mood and intentions, and can change the meaning of the words you use.

It's especially important to use a positive, welcoming tone at the beginning of a call, to make a good first impression and put the customer at ease. The first step in doing this is to smile while you talk on the phone. A customer can hear a smile in your tone of voice and smiling makes speech flow easier.

Different tones of voice and ways of speaking convey different messages. Someone on the phone may speak in monotone or in a voice that's low and slow, high and emphatic, fast and loud, or high and slow.

See each tone of voice for more information about how a customer may interpret it.

**Monotone**

If you speak with a monotone, you project boredom and disinterest, and the customer may assume you'd rather be doing something else.

**Low and slow**

If you speak slowly and in a low voice, the customer may assume you're depressed and you find it hard to speak.

**High and emphatic**

Speaking in a fairly high-pitched and emphatic or passionate voice shows the customer you're energized and enthusiastic about the subject. However, over-emphasizing points – or appearing unreasonably enthusiastic – makes you seem unprofessional and insincere.

**Fast and loud**

Speaking quickly and loudly suggests you're aggressive and possibly not open to suggestions or divergent opinions.

**High and slow**

Speaking slowly in a high-pitched voice may give the customer the impression you're doubtful, hesitant, or incredulous.

As well as maintaining a positive tone and adapting your tone to the content of what you say, it's important to use appropriate inflection. A lack of inflection in your voice makes you sound monotonous and dull.

On the other hand, using too much inflection in your voice can make what you say sound forced and insincere.

**Showing you're listening**

Active listening is crucial in all customer service, including the service you provide over the phone. You can give exceptional service only if you really know what a customer wants. So it's vital to listen carefully, both to what a customer says and to nonverbal cues like tone of voice. It's also important to prompt the customer to elaborate when necessary, and to confirm and demonstrate that you've understood.

Three techniques can help you listen actively. You should restate and summarize what the customer says, encourage the customer to tell you more, and demonstrate empathy by restating the feelings the customer has expressed in your own words.

See each technique for more information about it.

**Restate and summarize**

It's important to summarize the customer's main points in your own words. This lets you check that you've understood correctly – the customer can correct you or explain further if necessary. It also helps demonstrate that you've been paying close attention to what the customer has said. You can introduce a restatement of the customer's message using a phrase such as "So if I've understood correctly, you're saying that..." or "So the problem is that..."

**Encourage the customer to tell you more**

Whenever necessary, you should encourage a customer to provide you with additional information. You do this by asking specific questions that begin with the words "why" or "what." You may also use a direct statement that starts with "Tell me more about..."

**Demonstrate empathy**

Restating the feelings a customer expresses – or indicates through tone of voice – enables you to demonstrate empathy. It also encourages the customer to elaborate or to speak more freely. For example, if a customer sounds frustrated, you say something like "I know this can be frustrating for you" or "I understand how frustrating this is."

Tyrone recently purchased a new printer from a reputable supplier, but is having problems installing it in his home office. He calls Jessica, a customer service representative for the supplier, for help.

Follow along as Jessica takes Tyrone's call.

**Jessica:** Good morning, Sonical Group Customer Service, Jessica speaking. How may I help you?

*Jessica says, smiling.*

**Tyrone:** Hi Jessica. My name is Tyrone Oswald, and I'm calling about a problem I'm having with the printer I recently bought from your store. No matter what I do, it just won't print!

## Customer Service Fundamentals

*Tyrone says, irritated.*

**Jessica:** I'm sorry to hear that, Mr. Oswald. Would you mind telling me more? What did you do to install the printer?

*Jessica asks, concerned.*

**Tyrone:** I connected the computer to the printer by installing the drivers and checking the cable connections. I also bought a new cartridge to make sure that wasn't the problem. Nothing works! I've tried to connect the printer to two different computers, but it just isn't printing.

*Tyrone says, frustrated.*

**Jessica:** That sounds worrying. So you've tried it on two computers, with the drivers, and it has ink. What are you using to connect it to your PC?

*Jessica asks.*

**Tyrone:** I tried the USB cable, and the other one – that multi-pin printer cable. Both computers recognize the printer, but it just won't print.

*Tyrone says, frustrated.*

**Jessica:** Connection problems cause a lot printer errors, but it sounds like that's not the case here. Do you get any error messages when you try to print?

*Jessica asks.*

**Tyrone:** Nope. No error message. The printer just does absolutely nothing!

*Tyrone says, frustrated.*

**Jessica:** I understand how frustrating this must be for you and I really wish I could solve this over the phone. But I think the best solution is for you to bring the printer in so we can test it. If it's faulty, we'll gladly fix or replace it.

*Jessica says, consolingly.*

**Tyrone:** If that's what it takes, I'll bring it in. Thanks so much for your help.

*Tyrone says, hopeful.*

By restating and summarizing Tyrone's problem, Jessica makes sure she's understood the issues, and Tyrone knows she was listening.

She consistently encouraged Tyrone to tell her more about the problem which helps her find out as much as possible about the problem and its underlying issues.

Jessica also restated Tyrone's feelings in her own words, which makes her an empathetic listener.

Even though Jessica couldn't solve the customer's problem over the phone, her use of active listening skills enables her to give Tyrone excellent customer service – so much so that he's satisfied with the result of the call.

**Using customer-focused language**

If customers feel you're delivering responses by rote or failing to take their concerns into account, they're unlikely to be satisfied. For example, consider common statements like "Next customer please!" "I need your identification," and "You have to fax me a copy of the form before I can make any changes."

These statements are problematic because they don't focus on the customer.

A better approach is to use customer-focused language during all your calls. This language tells customers how your service will benefit them and it shows you're focusing on their needs.

Recall the previous, problematic statements. Now select each statement for a more customer-focused alternative.

**"Next customer please!"**

"Hi, thanks for waiting! How may I assist you?"

**"I need your identification."**

"Would you please give me a form of identification so I may assist you?"

**"You have to fax me a copy of the form before I can make any changes."**

"Would you please fax me a copy of the form so that I can make the changes for you?"

It can be easy during a call to default to self-centered language or impersonal greetings. However, if you maintain a focus on what's important to your customer, you'll make a better impression and find that the customer is much more helpful in return.

Now consider the scenario of Joe and Mimi, a customer service representative at an electricity supplier. Follow along as Joe calls Mimi to enquire about his recent electricity bill. Notice how Mimi focuses on Joe's needs and what she can do to help him.

**Mimi:** Hi , you've reached Brocadero. Mimi speaking – how may I help you?

*Mimi says, smiling.*

**Joe:** Hi Mimi. This is Joe Keenan. I've received an electricity bill that seems unreasonably high. Can you check this?

*Joe asks.*

**Mimi:** Of course, Mr. Keenan. Could you please give me your account number, so I can call up the details of your account and check your latest bill for possible errors?

*Mimi says, smiling.*

**Joe:** Certainly. It's 34424629.

*Joe says.*

**Mimi:** Thank you! There doesn't appear to be an error, but I notice your power usage has increased. We're in the middle of winter, so this isn't unusual. May I ask you some questions to find out how you could save money on your bill?

*Mimi says, politely.*

**Joe:** Of course, if it can save me money.

*Joe sighs.*

**Mimi:** What appliances do you use daily and at what time? Your answer may enable me to recommend a billing type that's more cost effective for you.

*Mimi says, smiling.*

**Joe:** Appliances?

*Joe asks, annoyed.*

**Mimi:** Yes, Mr. Keenan. If I know which appliances you use most at a specific time of the day, I may be able to move you to a package that costs less per unit.

*Mimi says, smiling.*

**Joe:** Oh, OK. I'm not home in the daytime, but at night, I use my laptop, TV, and microwave. Oh, and when it's cold – like during these last few weeks – I often use an electric heater.

*Joe explains.*

**Mimi:** Thank you! I believe you'll save considerably on your monthly bill if you switch to our nightsaver option. Basically, we increase your fixed fee slightly, but your night usage is billed at a much lower rate. You should give this option some serious thought.

*Mimi says, smiling.*

**Joe:** Wow, thanks Mimi! Please e-mail me the details and I'll let you know if I want to take up the offer.

*Joe says, happily.*

In a commonplace interaction like the one between Mimi and Joe, it's easy for things to become impersonal and for the customer to feel like he's got a raw deal. Mimi managed to resolve Joe's query to his satisfaction because she focused her language on him and his needs. He didn't mind answering her questions because she made it clear how doing this could benefit him.

**Helping resolve problems**

Often the reason customers phone is because they need assistance in resolving problems. So an important aspect of providing excellent customer service is your willingness to help your customers to the best of your abilities.

When handling customers' requests, it's important to avoid negative statements and to refuse requests outright, even if you can't solve their problem.

Take the example of a customer phoning about a delivery that is running late. As a customer service representative, you can't turn back time and make the package arrive on the due date, but if you offer alternatives, you can make the situation better.

By apologizing, offering compensation, or having your company absorb the customer's cost, you'll give your customer a good experience and salvage a potential disaster.

Tom is a customer service representative for an online book retailer. He needs to contact Trudy, a customer, to tell her the book she ordered has been withdrawn from circulation and is no longer available.

Follow along with Tom and Trudy as they discuss Trudy's order.

**Tom:** Good afternoon, Ms. Barnes, it's Tom calling about your order of the book "Suburban Sunrise." I'm afraid it has been removed from circulation and we're unable to get more copies.

*Tom sounds apologetic.*

**Trudy:** What? I've been waiting two months for that book! When I ordered it, it was available. I already paid for it!

*Trudy complains.*

**Tom:** I know you've been waiting, and we're very sorry about that. Apparently we received only half our order from the supplier, who ran out of copies. We'll refund you, naturally. Are you perhaps interested in something else by the same author? We do have his other books in stock.

*Tom says neutrally.*

**Trudy:** No, I don't think so. I've been trying to find that particular book for ages.

*Trudy says, annoyed.*

**Tom:** I'm sorry that we haven't been able to help you get the book. We'll send you a voucher as an apology, along with the refund.

**Trudy:** I appreciate that. Is there any chance the book may come back into print?

**Tom:** I'm not sure, but may I suggest you search for it on web sites that supply second-hand books?

**Trudy:** I didn't think of doing that – yes, thanks Tom. That's a good idea.

Tom found himself unable to deliver on what Trudy wanted, so he did the next best thing and tried to salvage the situation.

By remaining proactive and offering various alternatives, Tom manages to impress Trudy, even though she didn't get her book. So next time she's searching for a book, it's likely she'll return to Tom's company for help.

**Question**

A customer calls to complain about a delivery that hasn't arrived two days later than promised. The call reveals that, due to an employee error, the delivery was sent to the wrong address. A courier is currently on his way to deliver the article to the customer.

What responses exhibit outstanding problem–solving skills?

**Options:**

1. Apologize and explain why the delivery is late
2. Offer the customer a discount on a future purchase
3. Ask the customer to be patient until the delivery arrives
4. Offer the customer a complimentary gift to compensate for the inconvenience

**Answer:**

Option 1: This option is incorrect. An apology and explanation may help, but they won't do much to secure the customer's future loyalty.

Option 2: This is a correct option. Although you can't correct the mistake, you can appease the customer by offering a discount on a future purchase. This would help to secure the customer's future loyalty.

Option 3: This option is incorrect. Asking the customer to be patient may upset him more.

Option 4: This is a correct option. Although you can't fix the mistake, you can placate the customer by offering a gift to make up for the error. This would help to secure the customer's future loyalty.

**Mirroring your customer's language**

Mirroring your customers' language is an effective strategy for ensuring you use terms they understand and are comfortable with. This doesn't involve parroting a customer. Instead it involves picking up specific terms and using the same ones in your explanations to prevent misunderstandings.

Often adjectives carry different meanings for different people, so it makes sense to use the same terms as your customers if they use specific words to describe something.

Take the example of a businesswoman who phones a design company about creating a web site for her. She asks for a "vibrant" look and feel, but the designer reiterates her brief using the adjective "colorful." This holds a completely different connotation for the customer, and she feels misunderstood before the job's even started.

Another aspect of mirroring your customers' language is to match the style of their communication. Customers have their own personal style of communication, and you should try to match this style.

If a customer uses direct language, then you should speak quickly, organize your information before you speak, and focus on the customer's goals.

If a customer is chatty, you should speak quickly and energetically, allowing a little time for pleasantries. The key is to keep a balance between goals and unrelated chat.

Megan is a book review writer at a magazine. She calls Tom, the customer service representative for an online book retailer, to ask about a book that's due for release. Follow along as Tom handles Megan's query.

**Tom:** Good morning, you've reached Imagenie. This is Tom speaking. How may I help you?

*Tom says, smiling.*

**Megan:** Hi Tom. It's Megan. Can you tell me the release date of "Worth Every Penny" by Ramon H. Rosetti? A month ago, your web site had it down as August 30, but now it's September 15.

*Megan asks, frantically.*

**Tom:** Hi Megan. It'll take me a couple of seconds to check the release date on my system. So you're keen to get the book as soon as it comes out?

*Tom asks, smiling.*

**Megan:** I need to review it for an article on inspirational books, but if it isn't out until September, I won't make my deadline.

*Megan explains.*

**Tom:** OK, I'm just getting the results now. Which publication do you write for?

*Tom asks.*

**Megan:** BlazerFire. It's a magazine. Do you know the release date yet?

*Megan says. annoyed.*

**Tom:** I'm sorry for the delay. I can confirm that the book will indeed be released on September 15. Perhaps I can find another self-help book we're releasing sooner for you to review?

*Tom suggests, apologetically.*

**Megan:** That'll be too late. Also, I'm reviewing inspirational – not self-help – books.

*Megan says, worried.*

**Tom:** I'm sorry. I can take your name and e-mail address and then we can contact you if the date changes again.

*Tom offers.*

**Megan:** Thank you.

Tom failed to match Megan's style of communication. She clearly wasn't interested in small talk and just wanted a result. If Tom had sped up the conversation and just related the facts, he would have made a better impression.

Tom also failed to use Megan's language to describe the category of book she was after. If he had used Megan's term – "inspirational" – rather than "self-help," he would have avoided a misunderstanding.

# CHAPTER FIVE
*Customer Service Confrontation and Conflict*

**What causes complaints?**

Complaints from customers may arise for many reasons. Things go wrong, from late deliveries to billing errors, to product defects. All these problems can inconvenience and frustrate customers.

Have you ever had a grievance as a customer? How did this feel? And, if you complained, how did the customer service representative respond to you and what was the outcome of your complaint?

When things go wrong you're likely to feel frustrated. You might also be one of those people who delays making a complaint until your frustration has intensified into a feeling of anger. This is common. And it means many customers are already distressed and angry before they make contact with a customer service representative.

To avoid adding to customers' feelings of frustration, it's important that when you handle complaints from customers, you avoid certain common mistakes.

Customers often get more distressed when they feel that employees are trying to avoid responsibility for problems or denying that problems exist at all. Nobody likes to be contradicted or told to calm down, so customers generally don't respond well to this.

Another common erroneous response is to criticize your colleagues, your company, or your products or services to a customer.

You may make promises you can't keep in an attempt to placate a customer. When you do this, you set unrealistic expectations you can't fulfill.

Finally, some service representatives assume their customers are acting in bad faith. Being doubted in this way is upsetting for anyone.

So when you deal with dissatisfied customers, you need to avoid a number of common mistakes. These range from avoiding your responsibilities to assuming your customers are acting in bad faith.

**Avoiding your responsibilities**

When faced with an irate customer, it's tempting to try to avoid responsibility for a problem – or to shunt the customer to someone else. This is likely to frustrate the customer even further. Instead, it's important to be helpful, take ownership of the problem, and act as the customer's point of contact for resolving the matter.

See each guideline associated with taking responsibility for customers' complaints for more information about it.

**Be helpful**

You may be tempted to avoid responsibility, saying you're busy or you can't help resolve a particular problem. This unhelpful reaction will make the customer feel even more frustrated.

If you're busy when someone approaches you, promise to attend to the customer as soon as you can, and then deliver on your promise.

If you can't give exactly what a customer asks for, don't say you can't help. Instead, offer constructive solutions to the problem. Phrases that you can use include "I can..." or "I'll be with you as soon as I can."

**Take ownership of the problem**

When you feel accused or threatened, it's natural to get defensive. Maybe you react by saying there's nothing you can do, you don't know, or the problem is either not your fault or not your job to resolve. This knee-jerk reaction escalates tension. It also stops you from really listening to a customer.

Instead, you need to take ownership of the problem. If you feel you can't help, don't say there's nothing you can do. Rather find out if there's anything you can do to help. If you don't know the answers, say you'll find out.

If someone else needs to deal with a problem, let your customers know you're referring them to somebody who can help.

**Act as the point of contact**

When an irate customer approaches you, it can be tempting to pass this person over to your manager. This may seem like a good idea especially if the customer is asking for something that's not part of your company's standard procedures or you aren't sure what to do.

Instead, the best response is to reassure the customer. Then approach your manager yourself, and report back to the customer with a solution.

Now select each customer service agent to find out how he or she handles customer complaints.

**Sasha**

I ensure my voice sounds friendly and warm, because a pleasant tone goes a long way in setting a customer at ease.

"When I'm really busy and a customer is trying to get my attention, I often say something like 'I'll be with you in just a moment.' This tells customers I'll help them as soon as I can, so they are more patient.

When a customer asks for something that I can't provide, I make an alternative suggestion. I say something like 'What I can do for you is...' A partial solution is sometimes good enough – it shows I'm trying to help."

**Mario**

"Sometimes I'm not sure how to proceed or whether I can help a customer. At these times, I don't tell this to the customer. Instead, I say 'I'll find out.' And I make a point of doing just that.

Even when something isn't my fault or the fault of my company, it doesn't help telling the customer that – in fact it may make things worse."

**Melanie**

"When I first started answering customer queries at my company, I used to refer the difficult ones to my manager.

After a while, I realized some customers felt I wasn't willing to help them – even when my manager helped them straight away.

Now I say 'I can help you' to a difficult customer. I then ask my manager for advice and return to the customer to offer a solution. I now feel more confident and capable, and my customers are pleased. They're delighted to find somebody who's committed to sorting out their problems."

Sasha, Mario, and Melanie all make a point of taking responsibility for customers' complaints. The techniques they use demonstrate to customers their concerns are being taking seriously and they can expect professional, helpful responses.

**Overstepping your boundaries**

When handling customer complaints, you may overstep your boundaries in one of two main ways – by setting unrealistic expectations or by making inappropriate criticisms.

See each type of mistake to find out what you should do instead.

**Setting unrealistic expectations**

Making promises you can't keep to customers will only make matters worse. Even customers who aren't initially angry will be upset when you fail to deliver on what you've led them to expect.

To avoid this, first let customers know you understand the importance of the issues they're reporting and you'll do your best to help. Then make it clear what's possible. Try to negotiate a solution that benefits both the customer and your company, while being careful to offer only reasonable and realistic solutions.

**Making inappropriate criticisms**

Customers may be critical of your company, colleagues, or products or services. It's important you don't verify their criticisms or add similar comments of your own. This is inappropriate and unprofessional.

What you can do is apologize for shortcomings when appropriate and acknowledge a customer's frustration. You should make a point of finding out what happened and let the customer know you're going to do this.

You should also focus on possible solutions rather than on the problem itself or on how the problem occurred.

Lucy is a customer service representative for a software development company. Although she knows the company's products, she's not equipped to troubleshoot software problems. Follow along as she handles a call from Darren, a disgruntled customer.

**Darren:** At last! Do you know I've been kept on hold for the past 20 minutes?

*Darren is angry.*

**Lucy:** I'm so sorry about that. That's just bad service. Now that you've finally reached me, what can I do for you?

*Lucy is calm and speaks warmly.*

**Darren:** I've just installed the updated version of the accounting software from your company and now I can't access our inventory categories.

*Darren seems calmer.*

**Lucy:** OK. I'm going to do my best to help. I'm sure we can sort this out quickly and easily.

*Lucy sounds anxious.*

**Darren:** Great. Thanks!

*Darren is smiling.*

## Customer Service Fundamentals

Lucy apologized to Darren for the fact he had been kept on hold for so long, which was an appropriate response. However, when she went on to criticize the service her company is providing, she overstepped her boundaries and acted unprofessionally.

Lucy promised to do her best and focused on assuring Darren she'd help find a solution to his problem. However, she was wrong to lead Darren to expect an easy, quick solution when in fact she doesn't know for sure this will be the case. Setting up potentially unrealistic expectations like this may lead to further frustration and anger on Darren's part, especially if resolving the problem is more complex.

**Being rude to your customers**

Customer service representatives may be rude to customers, even without realizing it. Three important mistakes are telling customers to calm down, contradicting customers, and assuming your customers are acting in bad faith.

Asking someone to calm down can have the opposite effect. It can sound condescending and add to the frustration. Instead, you can use these defusing techniques to calm down agitated customers:
- allow customers to vent their frustration by listening carefully,
- show empathy and understanding of the customers' emotional reaction, and
- validate your customers' feelings.

When customers are clearly agitated and need to vent their frustration, it's important not to contradict what they're saying. So avoid saying things like "You must have misunderstood" or "We never do that."

Instead, use empathetic statements to confirm you understand the customers' emotional reaction and their feelings about the situation are normal and legitimate. For example, you might say something like "I understand how frustrating that must be."

If you make it clear you suspect a customer is acting in bad faith, conflict between you and your customer is likely to escalate. Instead, start by assuming a problem isn't the customer's fault and this person isn't deliberately misrepresenting the situation.

Don't prejudge your customers according to reputation or stereotypes of class, culture, or any other generalized assumptions.

Instead, try to give your customers the benefit of the doubt and cultivate an attitude of trust. This starts with a presupposition that your customers' intentions are honest and sincere. Even if customers initially appear unreasonable or even possibly dishonest, they may be acting perfectly reasonably from their own vantage point.

Catherine works at a call center. Follow along as she deals with Julio who's upset about his laptop's slow repair time.

**Julio:** I want to find out what's going on with you people! I sent my laptop in for repairs on Monday and it's Thursday already! I rely on that laptop for important work.

*Julio sounds angry.*

**Catherine:** Yes, I see.

*Catherine is sympathetic.*

**Julio:** Why haven't I got it back? It was meant to be fixed within two days. And why has no one told me what's going on?

*Julio asks angrily*

**Catherine:** I'm sorry you haven't heard from anyone. I understand your frustration.

*Catherine responds with empathy*

**Julio:** It's more than that – it's going to make me miss my deadlines. I'm not going to pay for this.

*Julio says forcefully*

**Catherine:** I understand why you're angry. Why don't you give me your ticket number and I'll try to find out what's going on with the repair?

*Catherine is calm.*

Catherine did a good job of being polite. She allowed Julio to vent, was empathetic, and validated his feelings. She trusted his motives and didn't assume he was simply trying to get away with not paying for work done. She tried to focus on solving the customer's problem, rather than arguing with him.

**Question**

Match the common complaint handling mistakes with the things you can do to avoid them.

**Options:**

A. Avoiding responsibility for a problem
B. Setting unrealistic expectations
C. Criticizing your colleagues or company
D. Telling a customer to "calm down"
E. Contradicting a customer
F. Assuming a customer is acting in bad faith

**Targets:**

1. Commit to helping the customer and act as this person's point of contact

2. Only offer solutions you know you or your company can deliver

3. Promise to investigate how a problem arose
4. Allow your customer to vent frustration
5. Use emphatic statements to show you understand how the customer is feeling
6. Always give a customer the benefit of the doubt and cultivate an attitude of trust

**Answer:**

To avoid the appearance that you and your company are avoiding responsibility, it's important to be helpful and to take ownership of customers' problem. Ideally, you should also act as their point of contact, rather than handing customers to someone else.

You should avoid giving customers unrealistic expectations by offering only solutions you know you or your company can deliver.

It's unprofessional to criticize your colleagues, your company, or its products or services to customers. So when customers complain, avoid agreeing with accusations or assigning blame.

Telling customers to "calm down" is condescending and can exacerbate their frustrations. Instead, allow customers to vent and demonstrate that you empathize with their emotional response.

Contradicting customers is rude and can escalate existing tension. Instead, validate the customers' feelings by listening and remaining empathetic. Also focus on solutions rather than on the causes of problems.

Prejudging customers or assuming their complaints are unreasonable or dishonest is unprofessional – and can worsen situations in which customers are already frustrated. Instead, give customers the benefit of the doubt and cultivate an attitude of trust.

**Defusing customer frustration**

What pushes your buttons and makes you angry? It may be a sense of unfairness, for example, or feeling your valuable time has been wasted. And when you're angry, what helps you to calm down? It's usually soothing to talk about how you feel and what has happened. But it's even better if you can solve the problem and remove the source of your anger.

When interacting with angry customers, it can be difficult to remain calm. However, following a simple process for handling complaints can help you keep your cool and be effective at resolving problems. This process includes four steps:

1. defuse the customer's frustration before proceeding, so the customer is calmer before you begin addressing the problem,
2. investigate the problem, ensuring you're clear on all the facts,

3. present viable alternatives for addressing the problem and agree on a solution, and
4. follow up to ensure the customer's problem is resolved.

An angry customer is likely to struggle to be objective. So, before you handle any complaint, it's important to defuse the customer's frustration. You allow the customer to vent, listen with empathy, and focus on the customer rather than on yourself. This sets the stage so that a solution can be found.

See each strategy for defusing a customer's frustration for more information.

**Allow the customer to vent**

It can be hard listening to someone who's angry. Try to remember the customer isn't angry with you and is just looking to resolve a problem. In other words, don't take it personally.

Resist the urge to interrupt or contradict a customer who's venting, even if you disagree. Confrontation is likely to anger the customer further and exacerbate the problem.

Your aim should be to allow the customer to vent so you can both search for a solution once everyone feels calmer.

**Listen with empathy**

Listening with empathy and understanding is one of the quickest ways to defuse a customer's frustration. This involves listening with an open mind, rather than assuming the customer is either unreasonable or mistaken.

You should also express your understanding and pay careful attention to details that may help you find a solution later.

### Focus on the customer

It's distressing to listen to somebody who's in the grips of a strong emotion, especially frustration. Your own emotions can prevent you from really listening. For example, if a customer is shouting at you, you may get flustered and fail to take in important information. So it's important you control your own emotions and stay focused on the customer.

You should avoid trying to form a response in your mind while the customer is talking. If you keep an attitude of caring curiosity, you're more likely to understand the customer. You also shouldn't deny the customer's feelings by saying you don't understand the problem.

Suppose a customer has been wrongly billed for a service. The first thing the customer wants to do is express frustration or anger. Only then is the customer ready to move on to the practicalities involved in resolving the billing error.

Don't make the mistake of taking the customer's anger personally. If you do, you're likely to get emotional yourself and may start reacting irrationally. You may respond verbally or nonverbally – expressing tension and impatience through your body language and expression.

Also avoid telling the customer to calm down. This is confrontational and likely to do more harm than good. It will come across as though you're trying to invalidate what the customer is saying.

Active listening goes a long way toward showing empathy and calming a customer. To listen actively, you first need to stop what you're doing and pay full attention. Then listen carefully, responding with connecting sounds such as "uh huh" or "I see" to demonstrate you're listening. Avoid interrupting with your own responses or trying to complete your customer's sentences.

Also listen to what lies beneath what a customer is saying. Ask yourself what the customer wants you to understand. Is this person feeling disrespected, for example?

Finally, gather any further information you need by asking clarifying questions. Then summarize what the customer has said in your own words to ensure you've understood correctly.

Tracy calls Thom, a customer service representative, about an insurance claim for her car. As soon as he takes her call, Thom stops compiling his weekly call statistics. Follow along as Thom now listens actively and empathetically to what Tracy has to say.

**Tracy:** My car was stolen last week and you aren't holding up your end of the deal.

*Tracy sounds angry.*

**Thom:** I'm sorry to hear that. Can you tell me what happened?

*Thom sounds sympathetic.*

**Tracy:** I visited a friend's house for dinner and when I came out, my car was gone.

*Tracy is unhappy.*

**Thom:** Oh no!

*Thom sounds kindly and concerned.*

**Tracy:** And now your company wants to tell me it's not worth what I paid for it? If I don't have a car, I can't work. I really don't understand why you're letting me down. I've been paying my premiums on this car faithfully for more than four years now.

*Tracy vents angrily*

**Thom:** Four years is indeed a long time! And I know how worrisome it is not to have a car when you rely on it to get to work. I'm going to do my best to help you.

**Tracy:** Um, OK. Thanks!

*Tracy responds with relief.*

Thom stopped what he was doing so he could pay attention to Tracy. He listened silently to let her vent her frustrations. He encouraged her to speak with the connecting sound "Oh no" in response to what had happened to her. He gathered information by asking her to tell him what happened. He then summarized Tracy's dissatisfaction, while expressing a desire to help. This calmed Tracy down and they can now move on to resolving the issue.

**Question**

How hard is it for you to really listen while a customer vents?

**Options:**

1. Not hard at all
2. Fairly easy
3. Very difficult

**Answer:**

Option 1: You say you don't find it hard at all to listen to customers while they're venting their frustrations. That's a very useful ability to have. You're probably able to listen to customers because you don't take their frustrations personally. Because you listen well, you most likely have a calming effect on upset customers and are able to help them effectively.

Option 2: You say you find it fairly easy to listen to customers while they're venting their frustrations. Remember, the better you listen, the calmer customers will become when they speak to you. To listen well, you need to be fairly calm yourself and you need to develop active listening skills.

Option 3: When you say you find it very difficult to listen to customers who are venting their frustrations, you're not alone. To help you listen to angry customers, try not to take what they're saying personally. You also need to use active listening skills to help your customers finish expressing themselves and move on to resolving problems. By developing active listening skills, you'll be able to stay calm and detached.

**Handling the complaint**

Once you've defused a customer's frustration, you can move to the second step in the complaint-handling process and investigate the problem itself. This involves gathering the information you need to understand the complaint fully and to identify appropriate ways to resolve it.

Select each employee in the service industry to learn what tips he or she has on how to investigate a customer's problem.

**Mario**

"I'm the manager of a busy call center, so I have to talk with lots of customers during the course of the day. When I'm investigating a problem that's been brought to my attention, I always ask questions about what is relevant. I try to ask enough specific questions to get a clear understanding of exactly what the problem is. If I need more clarification, I get the information from my team.

Getting sidetracked by irrelevant discussions wastes time and makes it hard to focus on the real issues. So I don't merely ask questions – I ask the right ones and get directly to the point."

**Catherine**

"Sometimes when a customer phones me with a request, I need to gather more information before I can assist. When this happens, I always apologize to the customer and explain that I need some time to investigate the problem. Then, instead of putting the customer on hold while I confer with my colleagues or do some further research, I offer to call the customer back.

This gives me time to investigate properly and I can control the timing of my next conversation. Another plus is that customers appreciate my taking the effort to call back and really feel like I'm taking responsibility in dealing with their problems."

**Melanie**

"I find it's good to remember that there's often more than one way to deal with any problem. So don't just grab hold of the first solution you can think of – aim to figure out a set of alternatives.

Not only can you present your customer with a choice, but you can respond more intelligently to new information and the specifics of each situation. You have more options.

Never say to a customer 'It's not my problem,' 'It's not my responsibility,' or 'There's nothing I can do.' This is upsetting and makes it sound like you're refusing to help."

So when investigating a problem, you should ask specific questions to keep the conversation focused. If you really need more time – for example to find out about a problem – you should offer to call the customer back. Finally, you should take responsibility for helping the customer by working to identify possible solutions.

The next step in the process is coming to an agreement with the customer about the best way forward. Can you think of guidelines for ensuring this process goes smoothly and leaves the customer satisfied?

It's always best to involve the customer in deciding on an appropriate solution. You should offer multiple alternatives when possible and check which the customer prefers. You can also ask the customer to propose a solution, although it's important you retain control of the conversation. Finally, it's important you set reasonable, realistic expectations about what can and what can't be done.

See each guideline for more information about how it helps you find agreement on a solution.

**Offer alternatives**

Offering alternatives and allowing a choice empowers customers and shows you're taking their preferences into account. Even when you can't give customers exactly what they want, you should offer alternatives where possible.

Try to come up with alternatives that are based on a sound understanding of the nature of the problem and on what your customers want. You can say things such as "What we can do is..." or "Which way would suit you best?"

At all times, avoid saying there's nothing that can be done or you can't help.

**Ask the customer**

You should welcome your customers' suggestions for ways to solve problems and collaborate with them in finding mutually satisfying solutions.

However, it's important you retain control of the conversation. You need to ensure the agreed solution is feasible and will suit your company, as well as the customer. You also shouldn't leave customers feeling they've had to resolve their problems themselves.

**Set reasonable expectations**

You should make certain your customers know what to expect from you and your company, and explain any relevant limitations.

It's always better to promise less and then deliver more than to promise more and deliver less. This strategy builds in a margin for error and ensures you can always meet or surpass customers' expectations.

Lucy wasn't able to help Darren earlier in the day. Darren tries the help line again later, and this time Catherine takes his call. She allows him to vent his frustrations with the poor service until he's calmed down. Follow along as she investigates the problem and resolves it.

**Catherine:** Can you tell me what happened when you installed the update Darren?

*Catherine is attentive.*

**Darren:** All our company's inventory categories were disabled. I installed it this morning and now I don't know what to do.

*Darren sounds puzzled.*

**Catherine:** Did you install the free trial version from our web site?

**Darren:** Yes. That's the one.

**Catherine:** Alright. That's where the problem is. The free download is a demo version and doesn't support inventory categories. If you uninstall it, your system will revert without any data loss. But if you want the latest version with all the functionality, you need to purchase it.

**Darren:** Well, I'm glad nothing's lost. But now I'm not sure whether I should install the full version or just go back to the old one. Why don't you explain to me the benefits of both options, so I can make a decision?

*Darren says concentrating*

**Catherine:** With pleasure. I think you'll be able to make a good decision based on the benefits.

*Catherine speaks with a smile.*

Catherine effectively identified Darren's problem and began to explore potential solutions with him. She asked specific questions without losing focus. Once she had identified the problem, she offered Darren a choice of feasible solutions, and welcomed suggestions from him without losing control of the conversation.

**Case Study**

Follow along as Trudy calls Sara, who works in a boutique, to complain about an incorrect delivery.

**Trudy:** We rely on your company to deliver our orders on time and to get things right. But you've sent all the garments in the wrong size. Why aren't orders checked before they're sent?

*Trudy sounds angry.*

**Sara:** We do check our orders. Tell me about the problem and I'll see what I can do to sort this out.

**Trudy:** This order couldn't have been checked. We ordered 50 extra large T- shirts, but we got 50 medium sized instead. We need the correct order this week for an

## Customer Service Fundamentals

important client and now your mistake is making our company look bad.

*Trudy sounds angry.*

**Sara:** I'm really sorry about the mistake. I can courier you the right size. The T-shirts should then be with you by mid-afternoon tomorrow.

*Sara responds with concern.*

**Trudy:** Alright, I think that may just work. I'll send the others back to you. But I'm not paying the postage nor will I pay the courier charges for the correct delivery.

*Trudy says, firmly.*

**Sara:** That seems perfectly reasonable. Let's find a way to sort out the best way to organize these deliveries.

**Trudy:** How about I give the courier the wrong order when he delivers the correct one? Then you can pay for both deliveries when the courier comes to collect the correct order from you.

**Sara:** That sounds good. Because you need the T-shirts urgently, I'm going to arrange things with the courier right away. I'll call you back to confirm everything's on track and let you know when to expect delivery.

**Trudy:** Thanks! We really need those T-shirts.

Question

What did Sara do wrong when dealing with Trudy's complaint?

**Options:**

1. She contradicted Trudy, and so failed to defuse her frustration

2. She lost control of the conversation

3. She went off track when she investigated the problem

4. She refused to help with Trudy's problem

5. She failed to welcome suggestions
6. She made promises that she couldn't keep

**Answer:**

Option 1: This option is correct. By saying "We do check our orders," Sara contradicted Trudy and created tension rather than defusing it. So even though the problem was effectively identified and a good solution was agreed upon, Trudy felt angry and upset for most of the conversation.

Option 2: This is a correct option. Trudy was still venting her frustration when they moved on to agreeing on a solution. So she was still confrontational when Sara offered to courier the shirts. Sara failed to empathize and then was too rushed to mention the cost of the postage. The result was that Trudy went on to make demands.

Option 3: This option is incorrect. In fact, Sara was able to identify the problem effectively.

Option 4: This option is incorrect. Sara offered some good, open-ended solutions. For example, she offered to courier the T-shirts.

Option 5: This is an incorrect option. Sara reassured Trudy that her demands regarding postage were reasonable. This welcoming response did a great deal to undo the tension caused by her earlier mistakes.

Option 6: This option is incorrect. By saying that the delivery could probably arrive by late the next day and promising to call back to confirm when they would arrive, Sara committed to getting the T-shirts to Trudy as fast as possible, rather than setting a deadline she couldn't be sure of meeting.

The complaint-handling process doesn't end once you've agreed on a solution. You need to follow up with your customer and on the problem itself.

You should call or e-mail your customer to find out how well the solution worked. If the solution isn't effective, you can begin another round of problem solving.

You may need to follow up on the problem itself. For example, a flaw within your company processes may often result in customer complaints. In these situations, you need to inform those who can address the problem so it doesn't occur again.

**Handling complaints effectively**

If a customer arrives angry and leaves angry, customer service has somehow failed. Customer complaints can be stressful to handle, but how well you and your company do this is a litmus test for the level of customer service your company can provide.

**Question**

What do you think are the benefits of handling customer complaints effectively?

**Options:**

1. Improving customer relationships
2. Having a positive impact on the image of your company
3. Showing customers you really care for them
4. Showing you're willing to make up for mistakes
5. Demonstrating excellent customer service standards
6. Reducing the cost of customer service to your company
7. Always giving customers what they ask for

## Answer:

Option 1: This option is correct. A complaint, if handled effectively, provides an opportunity to strengthen your or your company's relationship with a customer.

Option 2: This option is correct. When customer complaints are skillfully handled, your company earns a good reputation amongst the people that matter most – paying customers.

Option 3: This option is correct. Handling customer complaints effectively shows customers you care about their problems and their feelings.

Option 4: This is a correct option. When your company makes a mistake, handling complaints well is a good way of making up for it. You solve the problems that arise and your company is better able to follow up on its mistakes.

Option 5: This option is correct. Effective complaint handling processes are a benchmark of excellent customer service standards. A company that can't handle complaints properly can't serve its customers well.

Option 6: This option is incorrect. Good customer service requires the time, energy, and dedication of skilled employees, which represents a real cost to the company. It's a worthwhile investment in good customer care.

Option 7: This is an incorrect option. It's not always feasible or possible to give customers what they request. However, you should always offer alternatives that leave the customer satisfied and show you're willing to help.

Most large companies dedicate a great deal of effort to handling customer complaints effectively. It means they can foster good customer relationships, and earn a good image and reputation. It demonstrates real care for their customers and shows a willingness to try to solve problems. In short, it's a benchmark of excellent customer service.

# CHAPTER SIX

*Shaping the Direction of Customer Service in Your Organization*

**What are moments of truth?**

Good customer service is something that takes place between two people – you and your customer. In every interaction, certain moments will define a lasting impression the customer has of you and your company. These are called moments of truth, a phrase Jan Carlzon, CEO of Scandinavian Airlines, coined in 1985. Every moment that takes place in the context and the quality of a moment of truth depends on a number of factors, including the customer's mood at the time of the interaction with your organization.

More than thirty moments of truth may develop in any given service delivery scenario. Take the example of a restaurant – the first moments occur when the patrons enter the building and the last when they leave.

Along each step of the way, the customers will have moments of truth, for example when the waiter takes drinks orders and answers questions about specials, the time it takes for the drinks to arrive, and whether the manager comes to greet the table. How much they enjoyed the experience is certainly not only reliant on the taste of the food.

Moments of truth create emotional impact, so they leave a far greater impression than any technical details.

They can be positive, negative, or neutral, and some of them will naturally hold greater importance for a customer than others. These will then contribute far more to the overall impression than lesser moments.

If numerous negative moments of truth mark an interaction, this creates an overall negative impression. If a competitor offers the same product or service, but creates a good impression, it's obvious which one customers choose to return to.

Any leader or manager working with customers should be able to identify what makes a positive moment. Ideally, your aim should be to provide as many positive moments as possible to people who deal with your company, which will in turn foster customer loyalty.

Understanding what makes a moment of truth is really the key to understanding customer service. Your aim is to manage the customers' perceptions so as to reduce the gap between perception and the quality of service you provide.

Managing moments of truth requires a structured and systematic approach. First you map the customer experience, and then you research customer perceptions, take action for improvement, and review and evaluate periodically any actions you've taken.

See each step in order to find out more.

**1. Map the customer experience**

Mapping the customer experience involves breaking up the customer's interaction with your company into identifiable steps. You can then identify the moments of truth in each step.

**2. Research customer perceptions**

You need to research the data you collect about your customers' perceptions. You do this so you can devise a plan to create more positive moments of truth. Some of the methods you can use to research perceptions are to conduct surveys, revisit past customer complaints, and listen to employees' experiences.

**3. Take action for improvement**

Once you've identified areas and opportunities for improvement, you take action. You create better products and customer service processes, or provide appropriate training to develop the skills your employees need to create positive moments of truth.

**4. Review and evaluate**

It's important to review and regularly evaluate any actions you've taken. You do this because you want to find out if they worked and to stay in tune with the changing needs and preferences of your customers.

Effective management helps you to design products and services that impress customers, identify potential opportunities to raise your service standards, and recognize specific areas that need improvement.

**Question**

What are the important benefits of effectively managing moments of truth?

**Options:**

1. You're able to offer fast and efficient service from your employees

2. You develop customer loyalty by maintaining a high quality of service

## Customer Service Fundamentals

3. You can identify problem areas of customer service

4. You're able to discover what your customers perceive as quality service

5. You eliminate all negative perceptions of your product or service

**Answer:**

Option 1: This option is incorrect. Faster service from your employees may be desirable, but managing moments of truth aims to strategically fix all customer service problems.

Option 2: This is a correct option. The aim of managing moments of truth is to keep customers loyal.

Option 3: This option is correct. Effectively managing moments of truth involves identifying negative moments and taking action to create positive ones in their place.

Option 4: This is a correct option. Part of managing moments of truth is researching the customers' perceptions.

Option 5: This is an incorrect option. You manage moments of truth to increase positive perceptions of your service or product, decrease problems, and develop customer loyalty. However, you will never eliminate negative perceptions entirely.

**Mapping the customer's experience**

The first step of managing moments of truth is to map the customer's experience. Try to view your customer's interaction with your company as a journey and break that journey up into a series of segments. Each segment involves a number of different moments of truth.

Once you have broken down the customer's experience into segments, you can identify exactly which moments are crucial to them in each segment.

Take the example of purchasing a new pair of sneakers. You can break down this activity into five segments – you enter the store, pick out a pair, try the shoes on for fit, pay for them, and leave the store. During each segment, you and the assistant create moments of truth.

See each segment to learn which moments of truth it may contain.

**Enter store**

When you enter the store, the moments of truth are the greeting, the length of time before an assistant approaches you, the manner in which the assistant offers help, and how long it takes you to get to the correct section.

In the enter the store segment, the customer enters store, is greeted by assistant, asked the purpose of visit, and shown to the shoe section.

**Pick out a pair**

When you pick out a pair, the moments of truth stem from the assistant's actions. How well does the assistant know the shoe section? How helpful is he in suggesting prospective shoes to the customer? Does he know his stuff when it comes to finding the correct shoe for your chosen type of exercise?

In the pick out a pair segment, the customer looks at shoes, the assistant suggests various pairs and then asks more questions.

**Try shoes on for fit**

When you try the shoes on for fit, the moments of truth extend to the environment as well as the assistant's actions. Is the chair comfortable? Does the assistant create an easy atmosphere to try on shoes or do you feel rushed? Are the assistant's suggestions helpful? The main concern of this segment is how quickly and easily you find a good fitting pair of shoes that meets your specifications.

In the try shoes on for fit segment, the customer is led to shoe-fitting chair and tries on various shoes, and the assistant asks questions and suggests other shoes.

**Pay for shoes**

During the segment in which you pay for your shoes, the moments of truth take place in the context of the previous segments and also how long the customer must stand in line. The cashier's greeting and the speed and politeness with which the cashier processes the transaction are this segment's crucial moments.

In the pay for shoes segment, the customer selects a pair of shoes, goes to the checkout, and pays for the shoes.

**Leave store**

When you leave the store, the moments of truth are contained in the way the cashier says goodbye, so it doesn't feature high on the list of crucial moments.

In the leave the store segment, the cashier bids the customer farewell and the customer leaves the store.

The most crucial moments of truth in this interaction are linked to the customer's goal of getting the right shoes with as little hassle as possible. The assistant's knowledge of the store, the merchandise, and what's appropriate for this customer are as, if not more, important than a well-rehearsed greeting.

If the customer manages to find the right pair of shoes fairly quickly, a polite and efficient experience at the checkout counter is an excellent way to round off a successful interaction.

On the other hand, if the shop assistant is slow to help or the customer has problems finding a suitable pair, then the moments of truth in steps two, three, and four become negative.

**Researching the customer's perceptions**

After you map customer experience with your company, you should research the perceptions your customers have of your company's products or services to find out exactly what they expect from you. Only when you know what your customers want can you provide appropriate customer service training to your employees.

Various sources of information help you determine customer perception, including customer surveys, customer complaints, and employees' opinions and experiences.

See each information source to find out more about it.

**Surveys**

Surveys are useful tools for gathering data about customer satisfaction, but you need to design them carefully. For example, multiple choice questions can limit customers' responses, so you might miss out on important information you'd receive if you'd asked open-ended questions. A well designed survey tells you which parts of the experience customers found important and how they rated your service in those areas.

**Customer complaints**

Customers only complain about an area of your service they think is lacking or awful, so their comments are useful in identifying areas that need improvement. A problem with complaint forms is that many customers will simply not bother to fill one in, because they doubt whether they'll accomplish anything.

**Employees' opinions and experiences**

Because employees work with customers on a daily basis, they're able to observe a customer. Employees may pick up on tone of voice, facial expressions, and body language, and deduce what impressed a customer and what disappointed them in a way that a survey or complaint form couldn't have.

Using all of these sources, you should be able to gather enough information to paint a fairly accurate picture of your company's customer service abilities, and begin to identify the weak segments and negative moments.

Even if you can't remove or transform a negative moment entirely, you can still plan to soften the blow. If you have a customer who experiences an unfixable negative moment – a wrong delivery or broken product for instance – an employee with excellent people skills can often salvage the situation.

A sincere apology, an offer of compensation, or a helpful suggestion can sometimes turn such a negative moment into an opportunity to impress.

For employees to succeed in a potentially disastrous situation, they need to be familiar with the criteria for good perceived service quality:

- professionalism and skills to handle any situation,
- good attitudes and friendly behavior,
- customer accessibility and flexibility to cope with any problem,
- reliability and trustworthiness to take care of customers,
- recovery from problems, and
- a good reputation and credibility.

Take the example of a fast food delivery driver who brings a group of customers the wrong order. Even though this isn't his fault, he must bare the brunt of his customers' wrath. Select each criterion to learn how it relates to turning those negative moments around.

**Professionalism and skills**

Even when dealing with an angry or unreasonable customer, good people skills and a display of professionalism can calm the situation and lead toward a solution that will win them back.

**Attitudes and behavior**

A good attitude and customer-friendly behavior is vital to good customer service. Imagine how this situation could escalate into a fight if the delivery driver becomes rude or defensive.

**Accessibility and flexibility**

In this situation, flexibility is extremely important. In order for the driver to turn those negative moments into positive ones, he needs to be able to offer some sort of compensation or apology for the company's mistake.

**Reliability and trustworthiness**

Maintaining a high level of reliability and trustworthiness can be the difference between a customer perceiving such an incident as a rare slip up for a trusted company or business as usual for a fly-by-night operation.

**Recovery**

Closely linked to accessibility and flexibility, the company should have some sort of plan in place to deal with mistakes such as this and the driver should be aware of it.

**Reputation and credibility**

Dealing successfully with a problem will boost your company's reputation in your customers' eyes, because it proves to them you really care.

**Actions for improvement**

Once you've mapped your customer's experience and analyzed the data you've collected, what do you do? The most common course of action is to equip employees with the skills needed to create positive moments of truth and neutralizing – or turning around – bad ones. Or you can work on plans to improve your products and your processes to better meet customer needs.

It's important to be very specific with your training and improved products and procedures, because problems can occur in a single segment of your customer's interaction with your company.

If customers wait a long time before being attended to, or have to make a scene to get assistants' attention, then you need to fix this problem. Similarly, if the problem lies in specific processes or routines, you need to analyze and resolve these.

Take the example of a bank in which customers conduct transactions through tellers. You're a management consultant and you've have been asked to manage the moments of truth to help them deliver better customer service.

You've mapped out the customer experience and have gathered data about customers' perceptions. From this you deduce your employees working behind the information desk impress their customers by being friendly and efficiently. However, the tellers seem disinterested and unhelpful. The inevitable long waits compound the problem.

**Question**

Which plans of action will fix the problem?

**Options:**

1. Ask all employees to attend a brief customer service refresher course

2. Send the tellers to training to get them to work faster

3. Send the tellers to training to get them to act in a friendlier and more helpful manner

4. Send the information desk staff to training to get them to work faster

**Answer:**

Option 1: This option is incorrect. Clearly the tellers need training to create more positive moments of truth.

Option 2: This is an incorrect option. While speedy service usually impresses customers, the perceived problems with the tellers is that they're disinterested and unfriendly.

Option 3: This is the correct option. You've identified the problem area and can take the appropriate steps.

Option 4: This option is incorrect. Customers were impressed with the information desk employees, so the focus should be where the negative moments of truth occur.

**Reviewing operations**

After implementing a course of action to create positive moments of truth in place of negative ones, it's vital to review and evaluate your company's customer service regularly.

It has been said that change is the only constant, and this is especially true of customers' needs and feelings. If you rest on your laurels, trends will change and you'll find your business once again plagued by negative moments of truth.

Consider the example of an upmarket hotel catering to international visitors. The hotel's experienced a drop in reservations over the past few months. Management suspects this is due to the excellent customer service that the similarly priced and located competition offers. It decides to employ a consultant to manage the moments of truth for the hotel's customers.

**Question**

You're the consultant who's been called in to the hotel to assist in improving customer service. The hotel is quite well-known and has enjoyed a very good reputation until recently. Over the past two months, guests have begun making complaints.

Sequence the steps you'd take to help improve customer service.

**Options:**
A. Collect data through customer surveys and interviews with hotel employees
B. Implement a review system to keep tabs on any future slips in customer service
C. Implement a course of training for employees to fix the areas containing negative moments of truth
D. Map the guests' experience during a visit, divide the interactions into segments, and identify the crucial moments of truth in each segment

**Answer:**
Map the guests' experience during a visit, divide the interactions into segments, and identify the crucial moments of truth in each segment is ranked Step one. The first step in managing moments of truth is to map the customer requirements.

Collect data through customer surveys and interviews with hotel employees is ranked Step two. The second step in managing moments of truth is researching the customers' perceptions. In this scenario, it involves collecting data through customer surveys and interviews with hotel employees.

Implement a course of training for employees to fix the areas containing negative moments of truth is ranked Step three. The third step in managing moments of truth is taking actions for improvement. In this scenario, it involves implementing training for employees.

Implement a review system to keep tabs on any future slips in customer service is ranked Step four. The fourth step in managing moments of truth is reviewing customer service operations in case future problems occur.

**Customer service standards**

Consider a tertiary education institution that provides both full time and part time study programs, covering both business and creative studies. It's a market leader and has an excellent track record spanning more than 60 years. The institution prides itself on its mission to provide all learners with the best service standards and learning experience, and has developed a reputation for extraordinary service quality.

The institution's success can be attributed to its high customer service standards. It strives to meet the needs of all students – who are its customers.

To ensure it provides excellent customer service, the institution provides all employees – from lecturers to employees in administration – with adequate customer service training based on the institution's specific standards.

Employees take the standards very seriously and deliver excellent service consistently, ensuring they meet and exceed customer expectations, making them eager to return and do business again or recommend the institution to others.

Companies can create and implement a service vision and service standards, both of which are related to one another.

A service vision refers to the particular experience you'd ideally like to create for your customers.

Service standards, on the other hand, translate into concrete, tangible terms: what your organization and its employees need to do to create that particular service experience. When service standards are established and maintained, your customers can expect a reassuring consistency every time they interact with your organization.

An organization's service standards should be clear and easy for all to understand in order for all the individuals to work together toward the organization's vision. Effective standards are specific, action based, observable, and customer centric.

See each characteristic for an explanation of it.

**Specific**

Service standards should be specific so that all employees in an organization are aware of what exactly is expected of them.

**Action based**

It's important that service standards are based on action – everyone will know what needs to be done, by whom, and by when. No guesswork is involved.

**Observable**

If service standards are specific and action based, they're more observable, easier to quantify, and their progress is easier to track. Standards that meet this requirement can also be embedded into job descriptions and performance management systems.

**Customer centric**

In order to be effective and relevant, service standards should be customer centric. This means they should be based on the needs of your customers.

If you can meet the needs and exceed customer expectations, you'll lead the race in the competitive market.

Service standards vary from organization to organization, and all standards should be clearly communicated to all employees.

Examples of service standards could be to answer the telephone within three rings, to return customer calls within an hour and reply to customer e-mails within two hours, and to smile when you interact with a customer.

Or, your customer standards could ask for investigations into customer complaints and progress reports or feedback within one week of receiving the complaint.

Always bear in mind the difference between service visions and service standards. These are some examples of vision-like statements:

- always ensure you remain team oriented, and
- be customer focused at all times.

"Always ensure you remain team oriented" and "Be customer focused at all times" are vision-like statements because they're rather vague and general. They don't tell you "how to."

These statements are perfect for a customer service vision document, for instance. They communicate what employees endeavor to be, but they're not good examples of service standards.

Service standards tell you "how to" – what employees endeavor to do – and are specific, action based, observable, and customer centric.

**Question**

Which statements are examples of service standards?

**Options:**

1. Technicians are available for assistance 24 hours a day, 7 days a week

2. We guarantee rapid response to any queries or problems

3. All customers will receive service quotations within 48 hours of request

4. We strive to be a world class organization through our expertise and leadership

**Answer:**

Option 1: This is a correct option. This is a good example of a service standard, as it communicates what the company endeavors to do. It's also specific, action-based, observable, and customer centric.

Option 2: This option is incorrect. This statement is a service vision statement as it mentions what the company endeavors to be. It's also not specific about "how to" guarantee its rapid response.

Option 3: This option is correct. This statement is a service standard because it's specific, action- based, observable, and customer-centric. It's based on what the company strives to do, not what it strives to be.

Option 4: This is an incorrect option. This type of statement is a service vision statement, not a service standard, as it communicates what the organization strives to be. It does not communicate what the organization strives to do.

**Implementing customer service standards**

By ensuring the creation and implementation of effective service standards, companies can deliver customer service that's consistent. It's this consistency of service that in turn builds up and encourages customer trust and loyalty.

If you know what to expect from an organization every time you do business with it, you're far more likely to return with more business or even spread the word about its services to others.

An organization that's made up of employees who are committed to service standards has a better chance of being successful than one that provides unreliable, inconsistent service. If you're not providing a consistent service, you're creating an environment of customer distrust rather than one of loyalty and reliance.

At this stage, creating, implementing and maintaining effective service standards may seem like quite a daunting task. Where do you begin?

Well luckily there is a simple process that you, as a leader within your organization, can use to develop effective service standards.

In order to carry out this process, you have to follow three steps: identify what the service steps are identify what makes the difference between poor service and excellent service at each step, and convert the elements that make the difference into service standards

Frank runs a very successful guesthouse and prides himself on the excellent level of customer service he's maintained on a consistent level for the past six years. He has many loyal customers who return to his establishment year after year, and they've brought in lots of additional customers for Frank via word-of-mouth. Although his business is doing well, Frank is fully aware of the fact that he should asses, create, and implement effective service standards in his business.

**Drill Down Home Page**

Consider how you could develop effective service standards using the three-step process.

**Page 1 of 6: Identify service steps**

To start the process of creating effective service standards, you have to identify all the service steps within your organization.

Service steps simply refer to the separate instances in which customer interaction takes place.

Once you've identified the service steps, you should break them down further into sub-steps that make up each individual interaction.

**Page 2 of 6: Identify service steps**

In Frank's case, he identifies four instances when customer interaction takes place:

- guests make a reservation
- guests check in to the guesthouse
- guests make use of the appointed room and various facilities, and guests check out of the guesthouse

**Page 3 of 6: Identify service steps**

Frank then thinks about each of these individual service steps and breaks them down into sub-steps.

First he notes five ways in which guests can make reservations, each requiring or resulting in some form of customer interaction.

Guests can walk in to the guesthouse and make reservations in person, or call the reception desk. They can also make use of e-mail and fax, or make reservations online through Frank's web site.

When guests check in to Frank's establishment, they first approach the front desk area. Whoever is at the front desk greets them and asks for the name the reservation is made under or the reservation code. With this information, the front desk clerk accesses the specific reservation using the computer system.

**Page 4 of 6: Identify service steps**

At this point during the check-in process, it's necessary to ask guests for the deposit and to establish what form of payment they'll be using.

After guests have paid their deposit, the front desk clerk asks if they have any special requirements. Once settled, guests are then given their room keys together with directions to their rooms.

During their stay at the guesthouse, guests make use of their rooms and various facilities. Frank records six sub-steps to this service step.

## Customer Service Fundamentals

**Page 5 of 6: Identify service steps**

When staying in their rooms, guests may from time to time interact with housekeeping and laundry personnel when they clean the guests' rooms or collect and deliver their laundry. Guests may also interact with employees at the swimming pool or gym, the restaurant, or the front desk when leaving and returning to the guesthouse or collecting mail.

Properly managing each of these instances of customer interaction is essential to maintaining good, consistent customer service.

**Page 6 of 6: Identify service steps**

To check out of the guesthouse, guests are required to settle their accounts at the front desk. Guests arrive at the front desk and hand in their room keys. The front desk clerk then calls up their reservations on the computer system, prints out their accounts, and hands them over for the guests to approve.

If all is in order, guests make final payment for the stay before they leave the establishment. Sometimes, guests discover discrepancies in their accounts, in which case the front desk clerk resolves these as quickly as possible.

After identifying the service steps and breaking each of them down into sub-steps, you can move on to the next step in the process of developing service standards: identifying what makes the difference.

**Page 1 of 3: Identify what makes the difference**

Identifying what makes the difference is about recognizing what elements may add value to all interactions with customers that you've identified.

Enhancing the customer experience leads to greater customer satisfaction and, ultimately, a greater competitive advantage. Once you've examined and analyzed your service steps and related sub-steps, for each one ask yourself "What can be done to enhance my customers' experience?"

You should involve your employees in this process as well, because the most effective service standards are created when management and employees share their knowledge and experience on customer needs. This is because your employees often deal with customers on a daily basis and therefore develop a deep understanding of what your customer needs and expectations are.

**Page 2 of 3: Identify what makes the difference**

In Frank's case, all his employees, from front desk clerks to the housekeeping complement, are in direct contact with his guests, so Frank meets with them to get their ideas about what could add to great customer value.

For one, his employees mention that it can get very busy in the reception area, particularly when large tourist groups check in. To add value to the customer experience in this case, they suggest all front desk clerks make eye contact with waiting guests and assure them they'll be attended to as soon as possible.

Another point Frank's employees make is they've noticed when they respond in a timely fashion to guests who make bookings using fax, e-mail, or the web site, they receive very positive feedback from the guests. This definitely adds to the overall customer experience.

**Page 3 of 3: Identify what makes the difference**

Employees at the gym also mention they receive positive feedback when they offer their assistance to guests who are using the gym facilities.

They say that by simply acknowledging, greeting and assisting guests with gym equipment, they can tell that guests enjoy their workouts more and leave feeling very satisfied.

The front desk clerks mention they've received the same kind of positive attitude from guests when they make a point of greeting them and thanking them for choosing Frank's guesthouse when they check in and check out.

**Page 1 of 4: Convert elements into service standards**

So you've identified all the service steps in your organization and broken them down further into sub-steps. You've then used these steps and sub-steps as the basis for identifying the elements that contribute to a good customer experience. You now need to convert each of these identified elements into specific service standards.

Always bear in mind that in order to embed these elements into your organization, your service standards should be an integral part of all procedures, job descriptions, policies, and performance reviews.

You can also establish service standards by making them part of job descriptions and performance reviews, so your employees have to adhere to them.

**Page 2 of 4: Convert elements into service standards**

You need to make sure you enforce the standards equally. Unequal enforcement of standards will lead to them not being taken very seriously.

Also, when converting identified elements into service standards, always remain mindful of the fact that the standards created should be specific, action based, observable, and customer centric.

### Page 3 of 4: Convert elements into service standards

In Frank's case, he uses all of the elements raised in the meeting with his employees to develop effective service standards.

For instance, he decides to create a service standard that states if guests have to wait in the reception area for longer than ten minutes, front desk clerks should direct them to the guest lounge and offer them a complementary cup of tea or coffee.

Clerks should also ensure they check up on waiting guests every five minutes, assuring them they will be attended to soon.

### Page 4 of 4: Convert elements into service standards

Frank also creates a standard requiring all gym, swimming pool, and housekeeping employees to practice proper customer recognition with guests whenever they interact with them.

Another service standard he develops is in relation to correspondence from customers via e-mail, telephone, fax or his web site. He decides all correspondence has to be responded to within an hour of receipt, irrespective of the medium of correspondence.

### Case Study: Question 1 of 3

Claude's business has not been doing too well lately and he's getting quite bad customer feedback. This has prompted him to review his customer service standards.

Answer the questions in order.

**Question:**

The first step in the process for implementing effective service standards requires Claude to identify service steps.

How can he identify service steps?
**Options:**
1. He must analyze all job specifications
2. He should break down all customer interaction into sub-steps of activities
3. He needs to identify occasions when there's interaction with customers
4. Studying other businesses and identifying instances where they have customer contact

**Answer:**
Option 1: This option is incorrect. Analyzing job specifications is too general and may not provide enough detail and information that's required to identify service steps.

Option 2: This is a correct option. Once Claude has identified instances of customer interaction – the service steps within his organization – he should consider each interaction and break each step down into the sub-steps. These sub-steps are the activities that make up each service step.

Option 3: This option is correct. The term "service steps" refers to all the instances of customer interaction that take place with any member of staff within an organization. To identify these service steps, all Claude needs to do is pinpoint each occurrence of customer interaction.

Option 4: This is an incorrect option. Although studying other businesses can be useful, particularly when they're in the same line of work, it's essential that you study your own business as all are different and function differently.

**Case Study: Question 2 of 3**

Once Claude has identified the service steps, he needs to understand what makes the difference and adds value to the overall customer experience.

Which are convenient ways for him to determine what adds value to the customer experience?

**Options:**

1. He should ask his employees what their thoughts are about what makes the customers happy

2. He should ask his employees what it is that adds to their working experience.

3. He needs to analyze all service steps and think about what can be added to each one to impress the customer

4. He needs to analyze whether the customer service targets he set out for the previous period were achieved

**Answer:**

Option 1: This is a correct option. Once he's identified what his service steps are and broken these down into sub-steps, Claude should seek input from his employees regarding what adds value to the overall customer experience. Employees are in direct contact with customers, so they know what customers' likes and dislikes are.

Option 2: This is an incorrect option. Asking employees about their working conditions and what adds value to those conditions is not an effective way to determine what adds value for your customers. Your employees are not, after all, your customers.

Option 3: This option is correct. When Claude has identified each instance of customer interaction – each service step – he'll be better placed to consider each step individually and think about what could possibly add value to it and the activities carried out during that step.

Option 4: This option is incorrect. Checking whether previous service targets were met won't give Claude any information or details relating to what he needs to do to add value to the customer experience he wishes to create.

**Case Study: Question 3 of 3**

Claude now needs to carry out the last step in the process of creating and implementing effective service steps. This involves converting those service elements that add value to the customer experience into customer service standards.

Which approaches to converting value adding elements into standards work best?

**Options:**

1. Make the service standards created part of employee job descriptions

2. Evaluate customers' needs

3. Ensure that service standards are adequately reflected in all company procedures and policies

4. Ask employees for their input and feedback

5. Make sure company- and department-wide standards are enforced appropriately

**Answer:**

Option 1: This option is correct. The service standards that are created should be embedded into Claude's organization. This can be done by ensuring they're reflected in company procedures, policies, job descriptions and performance reviews.

Option 2: This option is incorrect. At this stage in the process, evaluating customers' needs will not help Claude to convert value adding elements into service standards. He should do this in the second stage of the process, when he's trying to identify what adds value.

Option 3: This is a correct option. In order to embed service standards into his organization, Claude must integrate them into all procedures, policies, and employee performance reviews, and enforce them across the entire organization.

Option 4: This is an incorrect option. At this stage in the process, asking for employees' input and feedback will not help Claude to convert value adding elements into service standards. He should do this in the second stage of the process, when he's trying to identify what adds value.

Option 5: This is a correct option. Not only must Claude integrate standards into all procedures, policies, and employee performance reviews, but he also has to enforce them fairly across the entire organization.

**Customer service strategy and focus**

Consider a tertiary education institution that provides both full time and part time study programs, covering both business and creative studies. It's a market leader and has an excellent track record spanning more than 60 years. The institution prides itself on its mission to provide all learners with the best service standards and learning experience, and has developed a reputation for extraordinary service quality.

The institution's success can be attributed to its high customer service standards. It strives to meet the needs of all students – who are its customers.

To ensure it provides excellent customer service, the institution provides all employees – from lecturers to employees in administration – with adequate customer service training based on the institution's specific standards.

Employees take the standards very seriously and deliver excellent service consistently, ensuring they meet and exceed customer expectations, making them eager to return and do business again or recommend the institution to others.

Companies can create and implement a service vision and service standards, both of which are related to one another.

A service vision refers to the particular experience you'd ideally like to create for your customers.

Service standards, on the other hand, translate into concrete, tangible terms: what your organization and its employees need to do to create that particular service experience. When service standards are established and maintained, your customers can expect a reassuring consistency every time they interact with your organization.

An organization's service standards should be clear and easy for all to understand in order for all the individuals to work together toward the organization's vision. Effective standards are specific, action based, observable, and customer centric.

See each characteristic for an explanation of it.

**Specific**

Service standards should be specific so that all employees in an organization are aware of what exactly is expected of them.

**Action based**

It's important that service standards are based on action – everyone will know what needs to be done, by whom, and by when. No guesswork is involved.

**Observable**

If service standards are specific and action based, they're more observable, easier to quantify, and their progress is easier to track. Standards that meet this requirement can also be embedded into job descriptions and performance management systems.

**Customer centric**

In order to be effective and relevant, service standards should be customer centric. This means they should be based on the needs of your customers.

If you can meet the needs and exceed customer expectations, you'll lead the race in the competitive market.

Service standards vary from organization to organization, and all standards should be clearly communicated to all employees.

Examples of service standards could be to answer the telephone within three rings, to return customer calls within an hour and reply to customer e-mails within two hours, and to smile when you interact with a customer.

Or, your customer standards could ask for investigations into customer complaints and progress reports or feedback within one week of receiving the complaint.

Always bear in mind the difference between service visions and service standards. These are some examples of vision-like statements:

- always ensure you remain team oriented, and
- be customer focused at all times.

"Always ensure you remain team oriented" and "Be customer focused at all times" are vision-like statements because they're rather vague and general. They don't tell you "how to."

These statements are perfect for a customer service vision document, for instance. They communicate what employees endeavor to be, but they're not good examples of service standards.

Service standards tell you "how to" – what employees endeavor to do – and are specific, action based, observable, and customer centric.

**Question**

Which statements are examples of service standards?

**Options:**

1. Technicians are available for assistance 24 hours a day, 7 days a week
2. We guarantee rapid response to any queries or problems
3. All customers will receive service quotations within 48 hours of request
4. We strive to be a world class organization through our expertise and leadership

**Answer:**

Option 1: This is a correct option. This is a good example of a service standard, as it communicates what the company endeavors to do. It's also specific, action-based, observable, and customer centric.

Option 2: This option is incorrect. This statement is a service vision statement as it mentions what the company endeavors to be. It's also not specific about "how to" guarantee its rapid response.

Option 3: This option is correct. This statement is a service standard because it's specific, action- based, observable, and customer-centric. It's based on what the company strives to do, not what it strives to be.

Option 4: This is an incorrect option. This type of statement is a service vision statement, not a service standard, as it communicates what the organization strives to be. It does not communicate what the organization strives to do.

**Developing a service strategy**

By ensuring the creation and implementation of effective service standards, companies can deliver customer service that's consistent.

It's this consistency of service that in turn builds up and encourages customer trust and loyalty.

If you know what to expect from an organization every time you do business with it, you're far more likely to return with more business or even spread the word about its services to others.

An organization that's made up of employees who are committed to service standards has a better chance of being successful than one that provides unreliable, inconsistent service.

If you're not providing a consistent service, you're creating an environment of customer distrust rather than one of loyalty and reliance.

At this stage, creating, implementing and maintaining effective service standards may seem like quite a daunting task. Where do you begin?

Well luckily there is a simple process that you, as a leader within your organization, can use to develop effective service standards.

In order to carry out this process, you have to follow three steps:
- identify what the service steps are,
- identify what makes the difference between poor service and excellent service at each step, and
- convert the elements that make the difference into service standards.

Frank runs a very successful guesthouse and prides himself on the excellent level of customer service he's maintained on a consistent level for the past six years. He has many loyal customers who return to his establishment year after year, and they've brought in lots of additional customers for Frank via word-

of-mouth. Although his business is doing well, Frank is fully aware of the fact that he should asses, create, and implement effective service standards in his business.

**Drill Down Home Page**

Consider how you could develop effective service standards using the three-step process.

**Page 1 of 6: Identify service steps**

To start the process of creating effective service standards, you have to identify all the service steps within your organization.

Service steps simply refer to the separate instances in which customer interaction takes place.

Once you've identified the service steps, you should break them down further into sub-steps that make up each individual interaction.

**Page 2 of 6: Identify service steps**

In Frank's case, he identifies four instances when customer interaction takes place:

- guests make a reservation
- guests check in to the guesthouse
- guests make use of the appointed room and various facilities, and
- guests check out of the guesthouse

**Page 3 of 6: Identify service steps**

Frank then thinks about each of these individual service steps and breaks them down into sub-steps.

First he notes five ways in which guests can make reservations, each requiring or resulting in some form of customer interaction.

Guests can walk in to the guesthouse and make reservations in person, or call the reception desk. They can also make use of e-mail and fax, or make reservations online through Frank's web site.

When guests check in to Frank's establishment, they first approach the front desk area. Whoever is at the front desk greets them and asks for the name the reservation is made under or the reservation code. With this information, the front desk clerk accesses the specific reservation using the computer system.

**Page 4 of 6: Identify service steps**

At this point during the check-in process, it's necessary to ask guests for the deposit and to establish what form of payment they'll be using.

After guests have paid their deposit, the front desk clerk asks if they have any special requirements. Once settled, guests are then given their room keys together with directions to their rooms.

During their stay at the guesthouse, guests make use of their rooms and various facilities. Frank records six sub-steps to this service step.

**Page 5 of 6: Identify service steps**

When staying in their rooms, guests may from time to time interact with housekeeping and laundry personnel when they clean the guests' rooms or collect and deliver their laundry. Guests may also interact with employees at the swimming pool or gym, the restaurant, or the front desk when leaving and returning to the guesthouse or collecting mail.

Properly managing each of these instances of customer interaction is essential to maintaining good, consistent customer service.

**Page 6 of 6: Identify service steps**

To check out of the guesthouse, guests are required to settle their accounts at the front desk. Guests arrive at the front desk and hand in their room keys. The front desk clerk then calls up their reservations on the computer system, prints out their accounts, and hands them over for the guests to approve.

If all is in order, guests make final payment for the stay before they leave the establishment. Sometimes, guests discover discrepancies in their accounts, in which case the front desk clerk resolves these as quickly as possible.

After identifying the service steps and breaking each of them down into sub-steps, you can move on to the next step in the process of developing service standards: identifying what makes the difference.

**Page 1 of 3: Identify what makes the difference**

Identifying what makes the difference is about recognizing what elements may add value to all interactions with customers that you've identified.

Enhancing the customer experience leads to greater customer satisfaction and, ultimately, a greater competitive advantage. Once you've examined and analyzed your service steps and related sub-steps, for each one ask yourself "What can be done to enhance my customers' experience?"

You should involve your employees in this process as well, because the most effective service standards are created when management and employees share their knowledge and experience on customer needs. This is because your employees often deal with customers on a daily basis and therefore develop a deep understanding of what your customer needs and expectations are.

**Page 2 of 3: Identify what makes the difference**

In Frank's case, all his employees, from front desk clerks to the housekeeping complement, are in direct contact with his guests, so Frank meets with them to get their ideas about what could add to great customer value.

For one, his employees mention that it can get very busy in the reception area, particularly when large tourist groups check in. To add value to the customer experience in this case, they suggest all front desk clerks make eye contact with waiting guests and assure them they'll be attended to as soon as possible.

Another point Frank's employees make is they've noticed when they respond in a timely fashion to guests who make bookings using fax, e-mail, or the web site, they receive very positive feedback from the guests. This definitely adds to the overall customer experience.

**Page 3 of 3: Identify what makes the difference**

Employees at the gym also mention they receive positive feedback when they offer their assistance to guests who are using the gym facilities.

They say that by simply acknowledging, greeting and assisting guests with gym equipment, they can tell that guests enjoy their workouts more and leave feeling very satisfied.

The front desk clerks mention they've received the same kind of positive attitude from guests when they make a point of greeting them and thanking them for choosing Frank's guesthouse when they check in and check out.

**Page 1 of 4: Convert elements into service standards**

So you've identified all the service steps in your organization and broken them down further into sub-steps. You've then used these steps and sub-steps as the basis for identifying the elements that contribute to a good customer experience. You now need to convert each of these identified elements into specific service standards.

Always bear in mind that in order to embed these elements into your organization, your service standards should be an integral part of all procedures, job descriptions, policies, and performance reviews.

You can also establish service standards by making them part of job descriptions and performance reviews, so your employees have to adhere to them.

**Page 2 of 4: Convert elements into service standards**

You need to make sure you enforce the standards equally. Unequal enforcement of standards will lead to them not being taken very seriously.

Also, when converting identified elements into service standards, always remain mindful of the fact that the standards created should be specific, action based, observable, and customer centric.

**Page 3 of 4: Convert elements into service standards**

In Frank's case, he uses all of the elements raised in the meeting with his employees to develop effective service standards.

For instance, he decides to create a service standard that states if guests have to wait in the reception area for longer than ten minutes, front desk clerks should direct them to the guest lounge and offer them a complementary cup of tea or coffee.

Clerks should also ensure they check up on waiting guests every five minutes, assuring them they will be attended to soon.

**Page 4 of 4: Convert elements into service standards**

Frank also creates a standard requiring all gym, swimming pool, and housekeeping employees to practice proper customer recognition with guests whenever they interact with them.

Another service standard he develops is in relation to correspondence from customers via e-mail, telephone, fax or his web site. He decides all correspondence has to be responded to within an hour of receipt, irrespective of the medium of correspondence.

As part of Frank's implementation of these service standards, he includes them in all job descriptions and performance reviews and develops them into key performance indicators.

**Case Study: Question 1 of 3**

Claude's business has not been doing too well lately and he's getting quite bad customer feedback. This has prompted him to review his customer service standards.

Answer the questions in order.

**Question:**

The first step in the process for implementing effective service standards requires Claude to identify service steps.

How can he identify service steps?

**Options:**

1. He must analyze all job specifications

2. He should break down all customer interaction into sub-steps of activities

3. He needs to identify occasions when there's interaction with customers

4. Studying other businesses and identifying instances where they have customer contact

**Answer:**

Option 1: This option is incorrect. Analyzing job specifications is too general and may not provide enough detail and information that's required to identify service steps.

Option 2: This is a correct option. Once Claude has identified instances of customer interaction – the service steps within his organization – he should consider each interaction and break each step down into the sub-steps. These sub-steps are the activities that make up each service step.

Option 3: This option is correct. The term "service steps" refers to all the instances of customer interaction that take place with any member of staff within an organization. To identify these service steps, all Claude needs to do is pinpoint each occurrence of customer interaction.

Option 4: This is an incorrect option. Although studying other businesses can be useful, particularly when they're in the same line of work, it's essential that you study your own business as all are different and function differently.

**Case Study: Question 2 of 3**

Once Claude has identified the service steps, he needs to understand what makes the difference and adds value to the overall customer experience.

Which are convenient ways for him to determine what adds value to the customer experience?

**Options:**

1. He should ask his employees what their thoughts are about what makes the customers happy

2. He should ask his employees what it is that adds to their working experience.

3. He needs to analyze all service steps and think about what can be added to each one to impress the customer

4. He needs to analyze whether the customer service targets he set out for the previous period were achieved

**Answer:**

Option 1: This is a correct option. Once he's identified what his service steps are and broken these down into sub-steps, Claude should seek input from his employees regarding what adds value to the overall customer experience. Employees are in direct contact with customers, so they know what customers' likes and dislikes are.

Option 2: This is an incorrect option. Asking employees about their working conditions and what adds value to those conditions is not an effective way to determine what adds value for your customers. Your employees are not, after all, your customers.

Option 3: This option is correct. When Claude has identified each instance of customer interaction – each service step – he'll be better placed to consider each step individually and think about what could possibly add value to it and the activities carried out during that step.

Option 4: This option is incorrect. Checking whether previous service targets were met won't give Claude any information or details relating to what he needs to do to add value to the customer experience he wishes to create.

**Case Study: Question 3 of 3**

Claude now needs to carry out the last step in the process of creating and implementing effective service steps. This involves converting those service elements that add value to the customer experience into customer service standards.

Which approaches to converting value adding elements into standards work best?

**Options:**

1. Make the service standards created part of employee job descriptions

2. Evaluate customers' needs

3. Ensure that service standards are adequately reflected in all company procedures and policies

4. Ask employees for their input and feedback

5. Make sure company- and department-wide standards are enforced appropriately

**Answer:**

Option 1: This option is correct. The service standards that are created should be embedded into Claude's organization. This can be done by ensuring they're reflected in company procedures, policies, job descriptions and performance reviews.

Option 2: This option is incorrect. At this stage in the process, evaluating customers' needs will not help Claude to convert value adding elements into service standards. He should do this in the second stage of the process, when he's trying to identify what adds value.

Option 3: This is a correct option. In order to embed service standards into his organization, Claude must integrate them into all procedures, policies, and employee performance reviews, and enforce them across the entire organization.

Option 4: This is an incorrect option. At this stage in the process, asking for employees' input and feedback will not help Claude to convert value adding elements into service standards. He should do this in the second stage of the process, when he's trying to identify what adds value.

Option 5: This is a correct option. Not only must Claude integrate standards into all procedures, policies, and employee performance reviews, but he also has to enforce them fairly across the entire organization.

www.ingramcontent.com/pod-product-compliance
Lightning Source LLC
Chambersburg PA
CBHW020903180526
45163CB00007B/2608